SPIRIT

OF

SHAOLIN

SPIRIT OF SHAOLIN

DAVID CARRADINE

Charles E. Tuttle Company, Inc.
Boston, Massachusetts
Rutland, Vermont
Tokyo, Japan

Published by the Charles E. Tuttle Company, Inc. of Rutland, Vermont
& Tokyo, Japan with editorial offices at 77 Central Street,
Boston, Massachusetts 02109.

Library of Congress Cataloging-in-Publication Data

Carradine, David.
    Spirit of Shaolin / David Carradine.
        p.   cm.
    ISBN 0 8048 1828 2 (pb)
    ISBN 0 8048 1751 0 (hc)
    1. Kung fu.   I. Title.
GV1114.7.C37   1991
796.8'159—dc20   91-65714
                                                  CIP

A portion of the royalties from this volume is devoted to the support
and promotion of Shaolin kung fu in the Americas.

Credits and Acknowledgments
Every effort has been made to obtain appropriate permissions and to
credit copyright holders. Rights holders who wish to contact the
publisher should communicate with the editorial office of Charles E.
Tuttle Company, Inc., 77 Central Street, Boston, MA 02109.

The passage on page 1 from Stephen R. Donaldson's *The One Tree* is
reproduced with the permission of Ballantine Books, a Division of
Random House, Inc.

Cover photo by Bob Kuhn
Book design by Janis Owens

Stance Drawings by Ken Hay

First paperback printing 1993
PRINTED IN THE UNITED STATES

Inspired and impelled by
Sifu Kam Yuen
without whom
it could not have been written

to Jeff
and all the rock benders

*This volume would not have been possible
without the aid, energy, and inspiration
of more people than I can name,
some of them dead for thousands of years.*

I am grateful to you all.

*I'm especially grateful to the world
for needing and wanting this book
to be written. That is your gift to me.*

I seek not to know the answers,
but to understand the questions.
Caine

To know is not what is important to us.
Even to learn is not so important.
What is important is to study.
The Sage

From the unreal lead me to the real;
From darkness lead me to the light!
From death lead me to immortality!
Brihad-aranyaka Upanishad

CONTENTS

BOOK THREE
THE LESSONS

APPENDIXES

There is a tale among us, a legend preserved by the old tellers from the farthest distance of our past. . . . It is said that upon the edge of the Earth at the end of time stands a lone man who holds the meaning of it all. . . . It is said that he has mastered all skill and prowess that we desire, all restraint and calm, and has become perfection—passion and mastery like unto the poised grandeur of mountains. And it is said, should ever one of us seek him out . . . and contest with him, we will learn the measure of our worth, in defeat or triumph. Therefore are we a seeking people. In each heart among us beats a yearning for this test and the knowledge it offers.

Yet the path which leads to him is unknown, has never been known. It is said that this path must not be known—that it may only be found by one who knows without knowledge and has not come seeking the thing he seeks.

You are that one.

Stephen R. Donaldson
The One Tree

David Carradine on location for "Kung Fu: The Legend Continues" with Nathaniel Moreau who plays his son "Peter". Photos by Gail Jensen Carradine.

THE
LEGEND CONTINUES

After I finished the first edition of this book and sent it off to the publisher in 1990, much has happened; and it has been suggested that I bring things up to date. Since the subject matter is more or less eternal, I don't see how that can hurt.

The problem is, where to start.

Well, the cold war had, so it seems, ended; the Infidel in Iraq had been traduced; the world had been swept by a new black plague called AIDS, which had put cancer on the back burner. The new American presidential race promised to be the most interesting in decades, and the Japanese economy showed signs of collapsing.

The Yugoslavs, with whom we had all had a whole lot of fun a few years ago, began systematically destroying each other, their country and their culture. A Holy war.

Several volcanoes had erupted. More people starved in various third worlds. (Isn't that an odd concept? Three worlds? There's only one, and we all have to live in it; even the real estate developers.)

Germany reunited itself; God knows what that will lead to. Quite a bit more of our precious rain forest disappeared. Hugh Hefner got married.

Probably the most interesting development as directly relates to this book is the beginning of a new syndicated television series called "Kung Fu, The Legend Continues." After several years of inter-office politics, this has become a reality.

I am sitting now in my new house in Mississauga, Ontario, Canada. I'm here because this is where (largely for economic reasons) we are shooting the series.

I have made a strong commitment to the success of this project, to the extent that I have virtually emigrated. I still retain my love for Thomas Jefferson and his American Revolution, and I have my absentee ballot; but, I am now essentially a resident of "Canadia."

They have built a whole new Shaolin temple for me here, and together we: myself, my fellow actors and my wonderful crew, are defying gravity and fate to put back together something that should probably never have been taken apart in the first place.

Our story takes place in modern times, and is forced to deal with all the madness that goes with it; but, then, that was always the point of the thing, wasn't it? Dealing with the madness.

Somehow, perhaps by miracle, we are managing to retain, and even expand upon, the eternal wisdom of the original show.

We have none of the old cast or the old crew on hand. Most of them are dead or retired, and we're in a foreign country where there are strict rules about foreigners taking jobs. Except for Mike Vendrel and Rob Moses, I am among strangers; but, Kwai Chang Caine has always been able to manage that.

It seems to me that there is more need than ever today for the ancient wisdom of kung fu. Violence, pettiness, idiocy and downright evil predominate our world; the media and the messages are garbled and misleading. The martial arts are being presented by the popular films of the day as brutal, calculated and geared for revenge! Nothing could be further from the truth. What we offer is a way to feel better, a path toward serenity, a way of peace.

More and more, as I study, I discover that the secret, and, indeed the strength, is in softness. Gentleness will prevail, just like Jesus told us. It's my opinion that this new series will teach us all even more than the old one did, which is saying a lot for anything as silly as a television series.

Keep your fingers crossed.

The earth is our mother.
She gives birth to all living things.
We must honour her to be worthy.
She is sacred, beautiful, strong and vulnerable.
She must be protected from her greatest enemy:
Her children of the human race.

Black Elk

Our rivers and oceans, our trees, all the animals and vegetables we don't eat, are being phased out. At the rate it's going, there won't be much left for our children, much less our grandchildren. At this moment, the planet is closer to ending as we know it than it has ever been since the demise of the dinosaurs. No, I take that back: since the great flood. I have, by some chance of fate, been given this opportunity to be a sort of Noah. Hear my plea: perhaps, in a small way, this little book can be of some help. I sure hope so.

David Carradine
Sherwood Forest
Ontario

SPIRIT OF SHAOLIN

THE TASK

 A few years ago, I received a message on my answering machine from Sifu Kam Yuen, my nominal Master for the last eighteen years. I called him back and he said, "David, I want you to write a book about the true essence of kung fu. As a result of all the movies that glorify fighting, everyone has got the wrong idea about kung fu. People associate it with violence and aggressiveness. They have lost track of the spiritual and philosophical aspects. I know, however, that you will never get around to it, so I'm going to write it and put your name on it. There is a great need for this book."

Every once in a while, the Master gives me a task, and I must perform it or suffer because of it. Yet, from time to time, I have taught the Master. We have grown up side by side.

So, I said to him, "Sifu, I have always agreed with everything you have ever said or written, but if I must do this task, I must DO it. Will you help me?"

After some thought, Sifu Kam Yuen agreed. "All right, David, but don't take too long. The world needs this book."

The task proved to be larger than either of us had anticipated. More than five years have passed since that day. At times Sifu almost gave up on me in exasperation. "Patience, Master," I said. "We have eternity."

"You may," he replied, "but I don't!"

There have been many influences in both our lives and in our art, too many to talk about them all in this little foreword. Let me just say that if I must write a book on the true essence of *anything,* I must first say that it is all *one,* and that all ways are *the way.*

I cannot limit my statements to those which are directly relevant to the martial art of kung fu because the essence of anything is the essence of it all. I will have to draw on my entire experience on this Earth to even approach the true essence of kung fu as I understand it. As I understand it, *everything* is relevant.

I'll try to tell everything I know here, but the subject my Master assigned me is kung fu, so there will be only a little about Jesus Christ, or my illustrious family, or Thomas Jefferson, or Ludwig van Beethoven, or rock and roll; not because I have anything against these things, they are all very important to me, but this book is about kung fu.

There are many other people more fit than I to write this book, but the task has fallen upon me. I am no Master of kung fu, nor a disciple, nor even a true student, by some people's standards. Yet, I have studied the Way of the Warrior all my life. In a way, my whole existence has been spent preparing myself to act as an evangelist for the art in its true form.

Well, here it is. For better or worse, as best I can do. We can do no more.

Yes, Master. So be it.

David Carradine
Sun Valley Ranch

CREDO

*Nobody ever said
it was gonna be
easy, baby!*
Boxcar Bertha

*Patience,
Strength,
Fortitude.*
Sifu Kam Yuen

 The purpose of this manual is to present the knowledge gained from Sifu Kam Yuen's thirty-five years of study and teaching in the art of kung fu and my eighteen-years association with his training methods, and from my training and studies for the role of Kwai Chang Caine in the *Kung Fu* television series and subsequent roles. I am writing it to fulfill the need to make known the true teachings and philosophy behind the art of kung fu and its relevance to the modern world. Much of the discussion is simply a reaffirmation of principles already known to all true martial artists.

At a time when the martial arts are being severely criticized for their violence, it is imperative to present the other side of their development—the positive aspects of the arts—and a blueprint to guide the seeker to these truths.

The real essence of kung fu is not self-defense but philosophy. What I'm going to try to deal with in this book is the true and real essence, so it will deal mainly with philosophy. If the reader is searching for a how-to book with illustrations of ways to deal with muggers and rapists, you've come to the wrong place. However, if you are a true seeker looking for meaning and significance, if you are on the road to enlightenment, then this book is for you.

The learning of the martial arts refines human

movement, improves skills, coordination, relaxation, utilizes the body more intelligently and prevents injuries, creates a life-long freedom of body movement, restoring the natural rhythms which modern lifestyles have inhibited. Kung fu offers definite techniques which can help anyone to achieve his or her full potential to become a complete person.

The confidence which the knowledge of body and space harmony can give the student will banish fear forever. This is the true nature of self-defense. It is a minor by-product of the true study of kung fu. Kung fu is a total way of life, of which personal combat is the least significant segment.

The spiritual part of the teaching will go far beyond the physical aspects of kung fu, enhance all those advantages and provide much more: harmony with and understanding of the true nature of the Cosmos we live in; triumph over most human problems—disease, misfortune and even death. There is no end to the student's potential gain. What you put in is what you get out.

Happiness depends on mental health and inner peace more than any outside factors. Kung fu study promotes inner peace, mental health, strength, fortitude, patience.

Kung fu is not a cure-all, and instruction can fail to instill these qualities. However, given that the burden is on the student, kung fu can bring happiness, long life, success, life without drugs or other crutches, self-awareness and self-confidence, freeing the mind to cope with outside forces more effectively, promoting understanding and eliminating confusion and frustration. Success in all endeavors follows.

True mastery of Shaolin kung fu cannot be accomplished solely through practice and study of exercises and dances. Nor can Sifu (the Master) be the whole source of information. This is good enough for the beginning or casual student, but inadequate for the serious disciple. The disciple must rely on himself and other sources to complete his information. Philosophy, religion, medicine, art, music, literature and science (especially physics) must be pursued until the seeker attains reasonably full understanding of these things. The disciple must make his own way. If this seems a lot to accomplish, perhaps one should re-examine one's goals to find if one has the will required to go on with the quest.

BOOK ONE

THE STORIES

David Carradine as Kwai Chang Caine in Kung Fu.

1

THE WAY OF
THE DRAGON

*How is it
you hear these
things?*
Grasshopper

*How is it
you do not?*
Master Po

 In the fall of 1971 something very special happened to me. I didn't know at the time how special. Nobody did.

I had just gotten back to town from making a movie in Arkansas called *Box Car Bertha*. It starred Barbara Hershey and was directed by Martin Scorsese. It was my first leading role in a movie. (Not starring, leading—there's a difference.) Saul Krugman, my manager and also an old friend, called me and said, "Look, I'm sending you a script for a TV movie. The only thing is, it has a series tied to it."

I said, "Saul, you know I don't want to do another series." He said, "Yeah, I know that, but I think you'd better read this script."

To give you a little background, my fascination for non-Western philosophy and exotic athletics began when I was about five years old, when I realized my big brother Bruce, who was the strongest boy I knew, and whom I idolized, was partly Native American. (We called it "Indian" in those days.) I noticed, was helplessly drawn to, and studied anything Indian from then on.

Just before I reached my teens, I became fascinated once again—with dancing. As I saw it in the movies. Judy Garland, Ray Bolger, Vera-Ellen, Dan Dailey. In school, every Thursday night we watched a

movie. It was always a western or a musical. The west-
erns thrilled me, but the dancers *were* me.

Back on the sidewalks of New York, I danced my
way through street fights and gang wars. I used my
lunch money to cut school and go to movies. I stayed
there all day. In the dark, on Broadway, at the Para-
mount or the Roxy or the Rivoli, I saw every Fred
Astaire and Gene Kelly movie there was. Then I
danced home after midnight, leaping past muggers
and weirdos through Central Park, dodging traffic
across Columbus Circle. My tap shoes made me bullet
proof.

I asked my father for lessons. He told me, "No
son of mine is going to make his living with his feet!"
I found money and took lessons secretly. They almost
ruined me. No great tap dancer ever learned from a
teacher. Bill Robinson? James Cagney? Ruby Keeler?
They all made it up. The best the teachers can do is try
to teach you to copy what they don't understand. I
survived the teachers. Even in the army I danced. At
Fort Benning, Georgia; Fort Bragg, North Carolina;
and Fort Eustis, Virginia, I was a star. I was twenty-
five then, dancing in an entertainment unit I'd formed.
When I was discharged in 1962, I was a lean and
mean killer hoofer.

I hitchhiked to Manhattan and found myself com-
peting with a lot of draft dodgers who had spent the
last two years getting ahead on Broadway. They
looked at my army haircut and my PX shoes and
laughed. I didn't mind the jokes. I knew who I was. I
had spent my last birthday crawling on my belly in the
mud of an infiltration course, with live machine guns
firing tracers over my head. I figured Broadway was
just another obstacle course. I was America's fighting
machine. These guys knew only casting couches and
unemployment lines. And then I had my Indian lore—
I had the Thunderbird on my back who was one with
me; I could change into the Coyote if I had to; I had
the Rattlesnake coiled around my arm; I could see

through the eyes of the Eagle. Broadway? Piece of cake.

Just before my twenty-seventh birthday, I opened on Broadway in a play about the conquest of Peru— *The Royal Hunt of the Sun,* in which I played Atahualpa Capac, the emperor of the Incas. This performance was my first great success. In it I could use everything I knew, and I did. I had been studying philosophy and history, developing skills as an actor and musician, and assimilating various physical and mystical disciplines.

Providentially, Jerry Thorpe, the man who six years later would produce and direct the original pilot for *Kung Fu,* was in the audience. When that story crossed his desk he thought of me.

For a few years I had tried to escape my fascination with the Third World by turning down those parts. I'm not sure we even had that term in those days: "Third World"—probably not. Then fatefully, one day, out in the woods in Arkansas, I decided that if there were some progressive function in society which I could perform by accepting these roles, and there seemed to be no one else to do it, and everybody else seemed to want me to say yes; well then, who was I to say no?

When the script, *Kung Fu, The Sign of the Dragon,* arrived at my door, I knew it was the one. Not because of the martial arts—none of us even knew anything about that. That was just the hook the movie hung on. It could have been basketball or downhill skiing. It was "the one" because it was a great story. It was about important things and it could make a significant movie, and it had that "Third-World thing" that I was looking for right then. The character of Caine was obviously perfect for me.

I had only heard the words "kung fu" twice before at that time, and knew nothing about Eastern martial arts except what I'd seen in movies and read about from time to time. I was, however, an athlete, versed in track and field, acrobatics and gymnastics to some degree, and had learned many Western martial arts disciplines: street fighting, guns, swords, knives, archery and quarter-staff. And I had some dance training.

It's possible that no one on the planet was as prepared on as many different levels to play the role of Caine as I was. Everything I had done up to that time pointed toward it in some way.

2

CHOSEN

Difficulty at the Beginning works supreme success.
I Ching

 I'd been working on getting this job for years without knowing it. But when it came down to it, it took me two interviews to get the part

The first meeting was with Jerry Thorpe, producer-director (he did *The Untouchables*); Alex Beaton, associate producer and destined to become the in-fact producer; Herman Miller, the writer, and later, story editor (who adapted for television the original screenplay by Ed Spielman, written six years earlier and left on the shelf in Fred Wientraub's office for lack of interest) and David Chow, the Chinese historical and martial arts advisor—a former judo champ and the man mainly responsible for instituting judo classes in California colleges. David was also an actor and a promoter—he was to provide us with the theatricality we needed to attract a jaded and uninformed public to the arts.

Jerry's office was in the old Jack Warner bungalow, which, I guess, was an indication of what sort of status he had on the Warner Brothers lot at that time. I came to the meeting with a shaven head. This was entirely by accident. I had shaved it off for an unrelated reason, though, of course, I wonder about that now. In *Boxcar Bertha* I had to shave patches of my head to put scars on and had to then shave other parts so I would look old. In the end, what I looked like was hell, so I decided to shave it all off. I passed David Chow in the hall as I came in, and he looked at me as though he were seeing a ghost. He told me years later that he had known instantly that I was the one.

I was told to sit in the office on the right and wait. Apparently I was early (an unusual thing for me). I asked someone where the men's room was and was directed to a black tile orgy room about the size of a tennis court, with jacuzzi and sauna and all that jazz. On the way back I passed a sort of board room full of busy assistants, which had giant crystal chandeliers left over, I was told later, from the days when Jack Warner used to use the place as a formal dining room.

I passed through this hubbub into Jerry Thorpe's inner sanctum and sat down in a brown chair in this totally brown office. I talked idly with Alex Beaton for a few minutes. Then a brown Lincoln Continental drove up and in came Jerry Thorpe. The room suddenly became a little darker. There was this huge man, dressed entirely in brown, with a Vandyke beard, looking slightly out of breath (well, as I said, I was early—he'd probably had to rush over from somewhere). His piercing brown eyes burned into me. I thought for sure he was the devil when I first saw him. I'm sorry, but that's what I thought. I never quite got rid of that first impression of Jerry. My loss.

Jerry Thorpe looked to be about the most powerful and dominating man you could hope to meet. This later turned out to be the absolute truth. He was a hard master. Determined to have his way, and used to getting it, he expected the maximum from everybody, and we gave it or suffered the consequences. Jerry was the rock on which the series was built, and the man who, through his personal courage, made it possible for me to achieve stardom. To this day, I would rush to his side any time he called.

The first meeting was very strange and inconclusive: I probably made a similar impression on Jerry to that which he made on me, what with my shaven head, and I think I had my dog with me. Now that I think of it, I was probably barefoot. I was already deep into the character of Caine.

Jerry did most of the talking. He told me how much he had liked me in *The Royal Hunt of the Sun* on Broadway, but we talked about the *Kung Fu* script just a little. They asked me how I was going to handle the martial arts part of the show. I said, "What happened to stuntmen? And, anyway, I think I can manage." For proof I jumped through the air and connected with the door jamb with both feet at a height of about two meters—really an acrobatic dance move, a relic of my boyhood fascination with Gene Kelly and Fred Astaire, but it convinced them of my ability.

The marks of my bare feet stayed on the door jamb for years. Meanwhile, I left without knowing if I had the part.

The next day, I got a call from my manager, Saul. He said, "What did you do in that office, for Chryssake?" I said, "What do you mean? What I always do. I just talked and acted a little like the character. Same thing I always do." Saul said, "Well, apparently you acted *too* much like the character. They want to know if you're a "crazy" or not." I blew my top. I said, "Look, if they don't like me, fuck 'em. Tell them to take their script and shove it." He said, "They *do* like you. They want you for it. They just want to know if you're gonna be reliable. Hell, I don't know. Look, they want to talk to you again. I'm gonna go in with you."

The second meeting was just with Jerry Thorpe, me and Saul. Jerry and Saul did all the talking. Things weren't going very well at first. I wasn't saying anything at all. I was sort of insulted that they hadn't said yes to me the first time, and I was really pissed off about the reliability thing or the "crazy" thing, whichever it was. I considered myself a clean machine.

Jerry kept pushing the point that this was going

to be a series, and the actor had to be ready to rise every morning at six A.M. and work hard for fourteen hours, every day, five days a week for five years. Then there was the question of cooperation, by which I thought he probably meant obedience (I had a reputation as sort of a rough customer). After a long, frustrating while, Jerry looked at me questioningly, hoping for a promise of some kind or maybe for me to grovel at his feet. I gazed at him inscrutably and growled, "I'm not gonna tell you *nothin'*!" As I said, I was sort of pissed off.

Jerry stared at me for a moment in shock, then turned to Saul and said, "I've changed my mind. He's got the part!" That was it. I guess he didn't really want someone who would grovel at his feet.

My two main competitors for the part were Bruce Lee and William Smith. If there was anyone else, I never heard about it. Bill Smith really seemed to want the part. He actually made a five or ten minute film for his audition, directed by Jack Starrett. I've seen the footage and it's brilliant, beautifully photographed, exotic, graceful and very cruel. Bill looks wonderful. He is massively powerful with a black Fu Manchu style mustache, and naked to the waist, muscles gleaming and rippling. Fierce. Terrifying. Completely unlike the thing we were going to do. He would have been perfect for *Conan, the Barbarian*.

Later on, Bill played an important role in one of the TV segments called "The Chalice." The fight we did together, with Bill swinging a massive chain, has proven to be one of the most memorable stunts of the series. The other one that the serious fans always mention is the walk in the rattlesnake pit. When they asked how we did that, I said, "they just didn't bite me." Actually, Greg Walker did the stunt (they just didn't bite him).

There are two stories about why Bruce Lee didn't get the part. One: that he was turned down because he was too short and too Chinese; which is a way of saying he was, ironically, a victim of the same prejudice we would be dealing with as our theme in the film. Two: that, for some reason I can't fathom, he was advised by his people not to take the part.

I was told by someone in the production company that they weren't sure he could act well enough to handle the complexities of the character. Maybe he grovelled at Jerry's feet. I don't know. Whatever the reason, it caused him to quit Hollywood, go home to Hong Kong and embrace his destiny.

Bruce Lee is thought of by many as a quintessential martial artist. Actually, he was first and foremost an actor. His father was a star of Chinese Opera. Bruce was born in San Francisco while his father was on tour there. He was doing work as a child actor in Hong Kong before he began his kung fu studies. The two disciplines progressed side by side throughout his life. While Bruce was possessed of great energy, concentration and charisma, the most memorable thing about him was his style, which was his own. Bruce studied the wing chun system, which is a very stiff style. He was prompted to develop his own system, jeet kun do, to escape the limitations of the style he was taught. He could have accomplished this goal simply by studying the flowing Northern Shaolin styles; but, then, we would not have jeet kun do.

Bruce was highly respected by the martial artists of the world, and he was dedicated to the art, but he was not superhuman. He was like us. He had his weaknesses and his blind spots like the rest of us mortals. He relied heavily on his right side, and his left was never as strong nor as fast nor as accurate. We know now that many of his moves were done by stunt doubles. These things in no way diminish the glory he achieved.

When he died suddenly on June 20, 1973, he was the number one box-office star in the world, and the first oriental actor ever to achieve international stardom.

There are many theories about the death of Bruce Lee. My theory is that he died for the same reason as did James Dean, Marilyn Monroe, John Lennon, Jimmy Hendricks, Amelia Earhart, Martin Luther King, Malcolm X, Anwar Sadat, and John and Robert Kennedy: He tried to grasp too much of the fire and it consumed him.

3

THE CORNER STONE

*Youthful Folly
brings success.
It is not I who
seek the young
fool;
The young fool
seeks me.*

*A spring wells
up at the foot of
the mountain.
The image of
Youth.
Thus the
superior man
fosters his
character
By thoroughness
in all that he
does.*
I Ching

 There was a series contract attached to the role of Caine. I couldn't play the part without signing up for the whole ball game. Five years they wanted. I definitely did not want to do a series, but I decided not to take that eventuality very seriously. It seemed unlikely to happen, considering the strangeness of the material.

During the shooting of the *Kung Fu* pilot, I told Jerry, "What I want is for this film to be so brilliant that it's too good for a TV series." He said, "Let's do both!" And I guess that's what we did.

We had no idea at the time that we were starting a martial arts explosion. We just knew we had a great script. You have to understand that none of us knew anything about the martial arts. The closest we had come was that we had all seen the Japanese samurai movies with Toshiro Mifune, when they had been popular, years before. I was a little closer to the source, but that's why I was playing the part. I knew exactly where to go in myself to find Caine. A few years earlier, while I was doing *Shane,* a series about a gunfighter, the producer, Denne Petitclerc, had asked me to play it as a samurai warrior. I knew exactly what he meant.

Kung Fu, The Sign of the Dragon was shot in twenty-eight days, in and around Los Angeles, during

Radames Pera in the role of Grasshopper (the Young Caine).

a bitter, cold spell, in December of '71. It opened with Caine, walking through the desert, somewhere in the Western part of the States, remembering his youth, particularly his early training as the first mixed-blood (he is only half Chinese) to be accepted to study kung fu at the Shaolin temple. As the action moves forward, with Caine entering into a town, and encountering rednecks, oppressed workers, and evil railroad men, Caine continues to remember his training and life in China. He thinks of his studies with the blind Master Po, who gives Caine the nickname of Grasshopper; of his eventual branding (with the tiger and dragon insignia, a mark of commitment); and of the day he must leave the Shaolin temple. Then, he remembers the incident that has caused him to be so far away from China. Years after Caine leaves the Shaolin temple, he runs into Master Po in the marketplace. Po is killed for an imagined slight to the entourage of the emperor's nephew (who happen to be passing through the marketplace). Caine avenges his Master's death by killing the emperor's nephew, an act which means Caine must leave China and spend his life running from those emissaries of the emperor who come looking for him in America.

We wanted the *Kung Fu* film to be as good as was humanly possible. In the interests of excellence and authenticity, we put together the greatest collection of kung fu masters ever assembled for a movie. One of these was Kam Yuen, who joined us to demonstrate the famous Praying Mantis form. Kam stayed to don a white beard and double Keye Luke as Master Po. Later, he doubled for me until I learned to kick for myself, and, in time, he took over from David Chow as kung fu coordinator. Later on, I took Kam for my Master, and we have become life-long friends.

At one point, after we'd been shooting for a few days, Jerry asked me to come to the rushes (the unedited film) of the previous day's work. I wasn't used to this kind of deference, or this kind of openness on

Keye Luke as blind master Po in Kung Fu.

the part of directors, so I told him it wasn't necessary, I didn't need to.

He said, "Please! We want you to see what wonderful work we're doing."

So I went. I came in late, and the first thing I saw was myself on a huge, twenty-foot tall screen. I was flying across the frame in a flowing, saffron-yellow monk's robe to plunge a spear into the heart of the emperor's nephew. This shot was quickly followed up by an eloquent close-up of Keye Luke as the dying blind Master Po. I was stunned. I knew we had a hit.

We finished up just before Christmas, all of us feeling enormously fulfilled. We knew we had been part of something great.

The picture made a big splash when it showed the first time, even though no one seemed to know what to make of it. Then, something happened which gave me my first hint that this thing might have a more far reaching effect than anyone thought.

It seemed that a lot of people hadn't watched the show the first time it was aired because they had no idea what it was. Now, they all wanted to see it. The network scheduled a second showing and, then, just when the whole country was tuned in to see this Chinese western they'd all heard about, the show was preempted by Richard Nixon shaking hands with Chairman Mao, to commemorate the acceptance of Red China into the United Nations. This seemed, to me, remarkably synchronistic.

The network cautiously ordered up four hour-long segments from us. They were to be shown once a month as a mid-season replacement. My contract didn't allow that. If they wanted to pick me up, they had to pay me for twenty-six. I was advised to hold the network up for a fortune, but I didn't want to do anything to stand in the way of this wonderful project. I had become a true believer; *Kung Fu* was no longer just a movie for me. I signed up without a squawk. Four great scripts were put together and work com-

David Carradine in a scene from Kung Fu.
© *1972 Warner Bros. Inc.*
All Rights Reserved.

menced at a luxurious pace of nine shooting days per segment, with Jerry directing. During this period, we established the search for Caine's brother, Caine took off his shoes and became a vegetarian.

In one of the segments, "The Dark Angel," my father created his continuing role as the blind Reverend Serenity Jones. This segment turned out to be a Carradine festival, boasting performances by my brother Robert, as Serenity's deaf and dumb assistant, and Keith, as the younger Caine.

John Saxon discovered martial arts in "King of the Mountain." Kam Yuen was the guest star of "Blood Brother," playing my old friend and fellow student from the temple. Kam and I started spending a lot of time together, and his quiet elegance, his simple, humble style—never forcing, never loud, erect and graceful—impressed me enough to cause me to change my portrayal of Kwai Chang to be more like him.

We discovered that I took to the martial arts moves easily and smoothly. We concentrated on what I did well, and stayed away from the stuff that looked awkward on me. Kam would say, "That kick is ugly. Don't you think that kick is ugly?" and we would try something else, then I'd go away and practice. Some things came to me instantly, without any practice at all—the three-sectional staff I got down in about half an hour.

During "Blood Brother," they brought in someone to double me demonstrating the White Crane, a difficult style to pull off, unless you happen to be a crane. The guy didn't look so good, so I took a stab. I had it right away. I was a natural, I was told. Well, I knew that.

There were so many letters coming in that the network changed its plan in mid-stream and told us to make fifteen more. We shut down to regroup without shooting the fourth segment.

Again, my contract was no good. Negotiations

began which never actually ended. The issue wasn't money; they paid me plenty. It was time. They wanted five years. I thought three was as much as I could give. We never could agree. I did the whole series without ever signing another contract.

We opened the real series with "An Eye For An Eye," the left over segment from the previous four. Jerry directed for pretty much the last time. He didn't care for the grind of the seven day schedule. It was a great show and Jerry won an Emmy for directing it. That season Frank Westmore also won an Emmy for his makeup and I was nominated for one—which is as close as I've ever been to anything like that.

Right at the beginning of this show, Jerry came up with the only solid piece of character direction I can remember him giving me in the whole series. He always left me free to do what I thought best. Like all the rest of the great directors I've worked with, Jerry's main methods were admiration and encouragement. No mind control, no coercion, no limitations imposed and no nitpicking.

The direction he gave me was, "David, don't act so heroic." That direction became the bedrock of the Caine character: extreme humility, total lack of conventional macho mannerisms and attitudes. As Master Kahn said to Grasshopper when it was time for him to leave the temple, "A wise man always walks with his head bowed."

This hint from Jerry also gave rise to the light touch of Stan Laurel in Caine, the "Little Grasshopper" who never quite grows up, and doesn't comprehend the society around him, walking through a wicked world unscathed, his innocence and cheerfulness being his main weapons.

As the season progressed, we were increasingly frustrated by the FCC's efforts at censorship, particularly of the fights. We would create an authentic, exciting sequence only to have it chopped up and watered down before it was shown. The FCC was especially

Philip Ahn as Master Kahn in Kung Fu.
© 1972 Warner Bros. Inc.

against Caine killing anyone. We had a staff meeting and decided to stop resisting and join them, making the sparing of life one of Caine's own major ethics. We weren't shaping the show, the world was. We also made liberal use of slow motion, reasoning that the softer look would have a better chance of getting past the scissors. We continued all along to have this censorship problem. We had become ABC's token non-violence show.

To complicate things further, the network wanted two fights per show, while the FCC limited us to four minutes of fighting. We solved this by having one short fight, usually early in the show, and one big one toward the end. We started working in extra training and practice sequences. They couldn't call that violence, and it still satisfied our lust for more kung fu moves.

I made a lot of TV appearances and did a lot of interviews—Johnny Carson, David Frost, Merv Griffin (with whom I did eight, we became old friends). Jerry told me when I started doing these, "Share the glory, David." I did my best.

The interviewers always wanted to know if I really knew karate. The name of the show was *Kung Fu*, but no one seemed to understand that it was the name of the art as well. I made no secret of my ignorance of kung fu. When asked, I'd say, "I know nothing." And then make some subtly dazzling move. I was being funny, sure. What I also meant was that what you see, what I do, though graceful, fast and effective, is as nothing compared to what there is to be learned. Not too many of the people out there got the point.

I still feel the same way about it. In comparison with all that there is to be learned, I know nothing. I think that no matter how long I study or how much I learn, this will always be my feeling. At one point David Chow told me that I knew more than I thought I knew. I knew enough to know that I didn't want to show anybody how little I *did* know. But, I knew more every day. Moment by moment, day by day, I was stepping more deeply into the arena that was Caine's. Sometimes I stepped surely. Sometimes blindly.

4

*The Gentle,
penetrating;
Wind and
wood.
Success through
what is small.*
I Ching

*If Kings and
lords could
harness it,
Heaven and
Earth would
come together.
Men would need
no more
instruction,
and all things
would take their
course.*
Lao tzu

THE
FLUTE

During a segment called "The Chain" an actor named Michael Greene showed me how to make a bamboo flute and gave me one he had made. Caine began carrying the flute with him somewhere along the way, though no writer or director saw fit to have me play it on the show until well into the next season.

A true martial artist must be well-rounded. Traditionally, the warrior should also be an artist. He should draw or paint, or make things with his hands, or play a musical instrument. This was my thinking when I introduced the bamboo flute into the series. They asked me on the *ABC Wide World of Entertainment,* "Why the flute?" and I told them, "Because it is important for a man to be soft." The flute is also an effective weapon, and a tool for meditation as well.

The *I Ching* has this to say: "The dark is dissolved by the penetrating light. The gentle wind disperses the gathering clouds, leaving the sky clear and serene. The tiny soft roots of the wood pierce the hardest rock, breaking up those dark intrigues which shun the light of day. All the while, the whispering music of the wind, and the gradual uncurling of the leaves produce tranquility and peace, appearing soft, gentle, unthreatening. The results of gentle penetration by the wind are less striking than the effects of

David Carradine as Kwai Chang Caine.
© 1972 Warner Bros. Inc.
All Rights Reserved.

aggressive force, but more enduring and more complete."

This principle, wielded by a warrior, is powerful and irresistible.

The flutes were made by me (part of the discipline). The bamboo came from the bamboo forest which grew beside the pond at Burbank Studios. I harvested the bamboo saplings and seasoned them by tying them in a bundle and leaving them, weighted with a stone, in Malibu Creek for a few months. Then I cleared the hollow centers and made the sound holes in the traditional way, burning them out with a hot poker. This must be done very quickly and lightly, a little at a time, or the bamboo will crack from the heat. The last step is a coat of clear lacquer inside and out, to protect it from the weather. This will also improve the tone. For extra strength, the flute can be wrapped with wet string or leather and allowed to dry.

The positioning of the holes, which determine the pitch, has to be done to a mathematical formula or the instrument will play out of tune. On the other hand, who says a meditation flute has to be in tune? Its purpose is not for playing "Yankee Doodle Dandy." In any case, little Grasshopper, there's always a way. I copied all of my measurements from a silver concert flute.

During one of the stories I demonstrated the making of the flute on camera. There were four different flutes in the series. I gave away all of them at one point or another to starry-eyed seekers I met along the way.

5

CHANGES
IN THE WAY

*Holding
Together brings
good fortune.
Those who are
uncertain
gladly join.
Whoever comes
too late,
Meets with
misfortune.*
I Ching

 We finished the '72–'73 season at the top of the ratings, with the blessings of the network and a no-strings deal for twenty-two more shows next season. "Same day, same time. Don't change anything."

On Chinese New Year, David Chow invited me to dine with the mayor of Chinatown. We rode at the front of the parade, and people cheered and threw rice. Barbara stood beside me, and I held up our new-born son, Free, dressed in saffron-yellow pajamas, for them all to see.

Around that time we began hearing rumblings in the East about somebody called Bruce Lee. Some of us were worried he would steal our thunder, but I saw something else: balance.

Back at Warner Brothers, others were hearing the rumblings too. Fred Wientraub, perhaps feeling stupid for having passed on *Kung Fu* as a movie, regained his losses by making a movie called *Enter the Dragon*. To spice things up, a competition karate champion named Chuck Norris was brought in as Bruce's opponent. So, in essence, one screenplay by a little-known occidental writer had ended up being responsible for creating the entire international martial arts explosion.

Enter the Dragon was required viewing for the *Kung Fu* executives and crew. After seeing it, Jerry said we were up against the James Bond of martial arts. I said it was more like the James Dean. How prophetic of Grasshopper. Anyway, we weren't up against it, we were part of it. Hell, we were the original.

Bruce was the yang, we were the yin. Bruce was fire and machismo, we were peace and humility. Together, we added up to a perfect balance, like the Beatles and the Rolling Stones. The movement grew and we mushroomed together.

We opened the season with a sizzling two-hour special, and just about everybody with a TV set watched us. Every actor in town wanted to be on the show, every writer wanted to write one, and every director wanted to direct one.

We just kept beating our old drum, by coupling excellent production values with historical accuracy, kung fu fighting, and Chinese wisdom. We documented redneck prejudice and gave an authentic chronicle of the difficulties of the Chinese people in America as East met West, with an occasional Black or Native American (or Armenian, for that matter) thrown in. Always fluid and shifting. Ambiguity was our metier.

Bruce Lee died. I changed the color of Caine's shirt from brown to saffron as a marker. We were alone again.

The *I Ching* says that "Holding Together" calls for "a central figure around whom others may unite." I wasn't sure I had the calling for the job, but, on the set, there was no way around it. I became the center of influence no matter what I did, whether I could handle it or not. In the front office Jerry Thorpe wielded absolute power with accustomed ease.

A power struggle of some kind was developing in the space between. Jerry and I were polarizing. It couldn't be helped. Unfortunately and unnecessarily, we had developed an adversarial relationship. We respected each other, even loved each other, but we didn't completely trust each other. We found ourselves constantly in opposition. I pulled hard to escape

Jerry's conservative efforts to hold me back from the radical plunge which he knew would take me right off a cliff, and which I knew was necessary for my survival.

We were both right and we were both wrong.

THE REVOLUTION

One day Jerry came to the set and told me he would no longer be producing the show. He was kicking himself upstairs to concentrate on his new series, *Harry O*. The show would now be produced by Alex Beaton, a beautiful man and a fine producer, who loved the show almost as much as I did, and John Furia, the story editor, who I hardly knew. I looked into Jerry's eyes and saw the terrible pain of lost love. I almost cried. He was abandoning us. He'd found a new lover. The show was never the same for me again.

All the writing, planning and hiring on the series had, by my own choice, always been done without me. I had a free hand on the set, and I made my views stick there. Then, John Furia tried to stop up that loophole and we tangled. The result was a revolution. I struck out at everything and everyone. John left, and Herman Miller rejoined the unit.

But these changes weren't enough. I knew this because I was the only person there who had any contact with public opinion, for the simple reason that people would recognize me on the street and come up and tell me what they thought. I'd been hearing from fans that there was too much judo on the show, and not enough kung fu. I, too, had become dissatisfied with the action as it was. We'd reached a plateau. I felt that David Chow had taken us as far as he could.

I got hold of Jeff Cooper, my friend and co-mentor since we came to Hollywood on the same plane in '63. He said, "It furthers one to see the great man, Pookey."

We loaded Barbara and Free into my old Packard Straight 8 convertible and drove out to talk with Dan Haggerty in the house he had built with his own hands at the base of the Santa Susanna Mountains. He came out to greet us with his two timber wolves, Masagwa and the Mother of Masagwa.

I showed him the fancy guitar that had been made for me by Stuart Mossman in Winfield, Kansas. Danny was there in Kansas when I made the deal with Stu, so I thought it would interest him. He took it in his gorilla hands and, holding it like a saxophone, he put the peghead to his lips and blew on it with all his might. He said, "It's got a busted reed!" and handed it back to me.

We sat down in front of a huge stone fireplace. I said to him, "What should I do?" Danny placed his hand on the head of the lion that was sitting quietly at his feet and said, "Be gentle, David."

The next day on the set was a fight day. This happened once or twice a week. David Chow would show up with a bunch of fighters, and we would make up a fight scene. This day, the fight was in a jail. Caine defeats the sheriff and four deputies as he breaks out of jail. Greg Walker had rounded up almost a dozen of the roughest, toughest stuntmen in Los Angeles, including Tony, Andy, and Gary Eppers, one of the Rondells, Buddy Joe Hooker, and Steve Burnette (the man who had taught me the fast draw, ten years before). Buddy Van Horn was asked, but he couldn't make it.

I took David Chow aside. "Let me do this one," I said. I brought him a chair. "You watch."

The rest of us got together and made up the roughest fight *Kung Fu* had ever seen. In between takes, I sprinted across to the other end of the lot to talk to Jerry. His phone would ring, the assistant director saying, "We need him." I would run back to the jail to do another piece of the fight then run back to Jerry's office and talk some more changes. This went on all day.

At one point, I was sitting exhausted on the floor with my back against the bars of a jail cell, catching my breath, when I felt a hand on my arm. It was Danny. He grinned at me. "I hear you're hot today," he said.

I would use no double that day. I insisted on taking real punches. I swung from a chandelier, riding it down once when it broke loose and flew across the stage into a plastic wall.

David Chow couldn't speak his mind to me. I was drunk with kung fu. He asked me "What do you want?" I said, "I just want it to be real!"

David said, "I don't mean that. What do you want?" I said, "I want it all!"

There was a stunt we had arranged where Caine jumps off a balcony and lands on the stone street in a fighting posture. We had a trick to make it work, but it was still a dangerous stunt. I wanted to do it myself. Jerry absolutely refused. Greg Walker, who had set up the gag, did it for me. Jerry and I watched it together. The handhold that was supposed to slow his fall broke off as Greg came down. He landed perfectly but very hard. Jerry said, "Six inches higher, and it would have been a broken ankle. The show would have to shut down for six weeks."

I said, "Jerry. I want to do it without David Chow."

Jerry replied, "Who will choreograph the fights?" I said, "I will."

He shook his head. "You don't have time. We can't spare you."

I said, "I'll do it on my lunch hour. I'll get some help from Curtis Wong and his brother."

Jerry shook his head again. "You can't do it all, David."

I said, "But, you saw it. It was great!"

*Kam Yuen as action double for Keye Luke as blind Master Po
in* Kung Fu.
© *1972 Warner Bros. Inc. All Rights Reserved.*

Jerry said, "Yes, it was, David. And if you try to do that every time, you'll break down. You can only do so much. You almost killed yourself twice today. The show would end. It can't go on without you." He waved his hand at the crew. "These people need this job. They have families."

I looked at Jeff. Jeff said, "Call Kam."

David Chow was my first teacher, and as such, will always have my respect. While his training in kung fu was incomplete, his spirit was great, and he shared his knowledge and love of Chinese culture with us all. The sessions we had together at the gym they built for us inside the courthouse on the Warner Brothers back lot, and at the house on Blue Jay Way, were the foundation of my training in martial arts. The kernels of wisdom he imparted to me still grow within me. His numerous contacts in the martial arts and the Chinese community brought much talent to light. More than once, David went to bat for us on some issue with real courage.

He lives now, as he has for years, in opulent luxury in "The House on Blue Jay Way" of Beatles' fame, and pursues many business interests, as well as his commitments to the martial arts and to the Chinese cultural movement.

Kam Yuen took over from David as kung fu coordinator, and real Shaolin and tai Mantis kung fu came to prime-time network TV. (The Praying Mantis style is Kam's specialty.) A couple of other people that the brass was sore about got the axe, and I had to take the blame for that, too. Every aspect of the show got a shake-up.

Still, I felt wrong. I asked Richard Lang, who had become my favorite director and a close friend, what I could do. He said I could fire Thorpe and take over as executive producer, and the show would fold for sure, but maybe I'd be happier. Richard was a funny guy. He and Jim Weatherill were the only two who managed to be utterly faithful and true to both Jerry and me through all this. So, I talked it over with Jim Weatherill, too. Jim was officially my stand-in, but his responsibilities far exceeded his nomenclature. He was responsible for getting me to work in the morning (he called it "rattling my cage"), and he was the one to talk to in any emergency. There was nothing he could not accomplish. He would go to any lengths to overcome opposition to our goals, including threatening bodily harm—to himself or others. At the end of the second season, he was named "Most Valuable Player." By the end of the series he had become the associate producer. Jim said, "Trust Jerry, Big Guy." I said, "Jerry's not here." He said, "Trust him, Kwai Chang. He'll be here."

The truth was, at that point nothing, not even Jerry's return to the helm, could have given me peace. It was a problem in my own internal soul. The show went on. Everybody still loved it.

The first day of Kam Yuen's fight choreography I knew we were on a roll again. The fight was great and *new*. Grasshopper never looked better. I was liberated, myself again. I arranged for Caine to lose his hat to mark the moment.

Kam Yuen was born Lian Kem Yuen, in Hong Kong, and, like all members of his family, began his kung fu training as a child. His Master was the renowned Tsou Chu Kai, acknowledged as the tai chi Praying Mantis of the World. Sifu Tsou Chu Kai was also an accomplished healer and was widely known for his technique of mending broken bones with deep massage. *His* Master, Mo Yuan, trained at the original Shangshon Mountain Shaolin monastery in Northern China and had the famous tiger and dragon brands, though not on his arms, but on his stomach—a rare mark of exceptional courage and accomplishment.

The animal brands were a traditional mark of commitment. In the pilot for *Kung Fu,* we showed Caine burning the flesh of his forearms on a kettle. We left out some of the details, because we didn't think

David Carradine and Kam Yuen.

anyone would believe them. It used to be that a disciple would have to go through a long tunnel to get to the cauldron. On either side of the tunnel, there would be all sorts of devices to maim or kill him. If the disciple got to the end of the tunnel—and, needless to say, there was a high attrition rate—he branded himself.

Kam is adept at most Northern and Shaolin styles, including tai Mantis, Law Horn, ling po, tai chi chuan, the Small Circular Fist, the Small Intellectual Fist, several Animal styles and virtually all the weapons: three-sectional staff, nine-sectional staff (or whip-chain), swords, double sword, halberd, knives, stars, wand and broom. I've watched him laughingly beat off a half-dozen attackers with a rolled-up magazine. He is also a gymnast, trampolinist and something of an acrobat.

With Kam in place on the *Kung Fu* set, we quickly began to approach a fully authentic portrayal of kung fu. To help the process out, I moved myself closer to the action, doing more of the actual stunts than I ever had. At the start of the third season, I started formally studying kung fu. I began working out with an instructor from the school that Kam ran. I worked with the instructor for several hours every day. By then, I was finished forever with fight doubles. My stunt double, Greg Walker, moved up to become the stunt coordinator and only stepped in to jump off buildings for me—or to walk through fire. (In movies a chair that will break into pieces when you hit it over somebody's head is called a "breakaway chair." We used to call Greg "the breakaway Caine.")

During the third season, I also changed Caine's costume to a classic black silk gung fu outfit. We did a lot of great shows that year, including a two-parter which took place entirely in the Shaolin temple in China. I got to direct that one. I cast Barbara Hershey to play opposite me as a female gung fu master with whom Caine falls in love. She dies tragically at the end. Victor Sen Young, who was one of the absolute best Asian actors and a hero in real life, played a renegade Master who was her teacher. Victor is dead now, God rest his soul, as are Keye Luke, Philip Ahn, Richard Loo, Benson Fong, Frank Westmore and so many of my dear friends from the show, as well as my father, whose guidance and inspiration have sustained me throughout my life.

7

THE WRITING
ON THE WALL

▬▬ ▬▬
▬ ▬▬ When my directorial turn was over, I could
▬▬ ▬▬ see how poorly my relations with the crew,
▬▬ ▬▬ the studio, and the network had become. I
▬▬▬▬ had been too hard for too long, screamed in
anger at too many people and stayed too much to
myself. Morale was irreparably low. Jerry, Alex and
Herman had a meeting in my trailer and Jerry pointed
out what the network was doing with our work—putting it in a different time slot every week to bolster up
failing ratings on other shows. "Cannon fodder" was
what he called it. I felt if that was all they thought of
us, maybe it was time to close up shop. The guys
agreed. No one was having much fun anymore, and
we all needed to get on to other things. The network
said they'd have to think about it. I told them to look
at the contract. (Remember, I didn't have one.)

We finished up with a five-hour marathon show
in which Kwai Chang finally found his brother, and
little Grasshopper walked off into the sun for the last
time. That show was so good we almost reconsidered,
but the die was cast. We threw in one more for nostalgia's sake, bringing back my father's blind Serenity
Jones for one last time. Everybody was tearful and
loving at the end, and again we wavered, but I had
always sworn that the third year would be the last. At
the end of the season, on February 5, 1975, I walked.

*And having
writ, moves on.
Nor all your
tears, nor all
your piety,
Can cancel
scarcely half a
line.*
Omar
Khayyám

*He who knows
he has enough
is rich.
To die but not
to perish
Is to be eternally
present.
One must know
when to stop.*
Lao tzu

We'd completed sixty-two segments in addition to the pilot film. I'd missed altogether one-and-a-half days of work, out of a possible four-hundred-sixty-eight (so much for the reliability factor), and I'd broken or dislocated every finger and toe at least once. I'd lost my family and spent my fortune and broken off with just about every friend I had. I was in superb physical condition and totally shattered emotionally—ripe for rebirth.

I assumed that was the end of me and martial arts, but I had underestimated both myself and the spirit of Shaolin.

8

AFTER THE FALL

Work on What Has Been Spoiled has supreme success.

The Turning Point. It furthers one to have someplace to go. I Ching

Two weeks after I left the series, I went right into *Death Race 2000* in a deliberate move to kill the image of Caine and launch a movie career. The movie career part was firmly secured a few months later with *Bound for Glory,* arguably my best role to date. Killing Kwai Chang Caine was another matter.

Early in '76, I settled down to a regimen of running on the beach. I worked my way up to seven miles a day, but in slow motion. I was a strict vegan vegetarian, consumed no drugs of any kind, kept my house clean, and went to bed early. I did a lot of reading. My only associations were my twelve-year-old daughter, Calista, and my dog, Buffalo.

One Saturday morning, while relaxing on the beach, I spontaneously fell into a state of meditation. When I came to I jumped up, vaulted into my yellow Ferrari, drove as fast as was possible to Torrance, a distance of about forty miles, and walked into Kam Yuen's 11:00 class. Kam was very surprised. He hadn't expected ever to see me again.

He gave me a key to the kwoon (the place where students practice), and for a while I lived in a little room at the back. I spent my days sweeping the gym, and working out, eating health food from the company store and talking with fellow martial artists. I was living the pure, holy existence of a Shaolin monk.

Then, one night, I went out on a date. I lost the key to the kwoon somewhere on Mulholland Drive. Kam never gave me another. I moved in with the girl, and that was the end of my life at the kwoon. Women have always been my downfall.

I continued working out with Sifu Kam Yuen daily at home in my backyard, learning new forms and techniques. I started into tai chi chuan, and began working the ling po form, got into the nine-sectional staff, also known as the whip-chain. Kam gave me a very special nine-sectional and a three-sectional, both made in the People's Republic. I still have them.

About this time, I started what was to be a long, concerted effort to bring to the screen a movie about kung fu called *The Silent Flute*.

9

THE THREE TRIALS

Tie two birds together; Though they have four wings, They cannot fly.
Ah Sahm

The Silent Flute, or *Circle of Iron,* as it was finally called, was a story for a movie which would, at long last, present the true essence of kung fu. The idea for it was generated by Bruce Lee while he was still in Hollywood. He had help from two of his students: James Coburn, the actor, and Stirling Silliphant, the creator-writer-producer who was responsible for *Route 66.* In the story, the Seeker, Cord, must survive three trials in order to reach his goal, which is to confront Zetan, the legendary keeper of the Book which contains all knowledge. As he makes his way toward Zetan, he hears the tinkling of a bell. It is a bell on the toe of Ah Sahm, a blind Master of incredible fighting skill. Reluctantly, the blind man becomes Cord's teacher. The plan was for Coburn to play the Seeker and for Bruce to play more or less all the other parts: the Blind Master and the Three Trials. Stirling was to be responsible for the screenplay. However, Bruce died without making the film.

John Drew Barrymore (the son of the famous actor, and father of the child star Drew Barrymore), was close to James Coburn. He obtained a copy of the screenplay from Jim's bookcase and brought it to me.

I could not get that script out of my thoughts. It seemed to me vitally important that the movie get made. The story and treatment were right on the cutting edge of what it's really all about. In some ways, the script was a lot like the original *Kung Fu* screenplay, the one that had languished in Fred Wientraub's office for so long. Like that script, *The Silent Flute* was too radical for the studios to consider. As extreme as it was, it was not hard to see why it hadn't been made. There was also, of course, the problem of casting. Jim Coburn was much older and afflicted with crippling arthritis, and Bruce was definitely unavailable.

I was perfect for Cord, the Seeker, and, with my reputation, I was sure I could get the picture made, but if I played Cord, who was there out there who could play Bruce?

It came to me that if I took over for Bruce as Ah Sahm (the blind Master), the Monkey King, the Panther Man, and Changsha (the Earth Power), it might be easier to find another Seeker. Actually, one came to mind immediately: my old friend and philosophical sparring partner, Jeff Cooper. Jeff was also a student of Kam Yuen and a martial arts star in his own right. Jeff was the one man on the Earth I was physically afraid of, and the one I would most trust with my back. It seemed perfect, made in heaven. I started devoting myself to putting it together.

To this end I stepped up my kung fu studies. Sifu went with me everywhere now, and we worked out all day, every day, whenever we could. We were not only practicing techniques, but also forging ahead onto fresh ground and beginning to establish the direction the fights would go.

I had to have four distinct styles in the movie, so my work was cut out for me. I started working on the Monkey King style, perfected my butterfly kick, added some flashy new spinning kicks, learned some "Old Man" techniques, and worked hard and long to increase my strength, endurance, precision, speed and accuracy. I practiced with the long staff, got down some gymnastics moves and spent many hours on a trampoline. Meanwhile, during office hours, I exercised my extremely minimal movie-mogul abilities to try to get a deal set to make the picture. Finally, *The Silent Flute* and I ended up with a producer named Sandy Howard.

Sandy was hot to have me play Cord, the Seeker. I said "Look. I've already played that part. I've been doing it for five years. It's time for me to play the teacher, and, anyway, who can we find to play Bruce Lee's parts?"

He said, "We'll get a bunch of guys: Alec Guinness for Ah Sahm, Oliver Reed or Omar Sharif for Changsha, etc., and then we'll just double them in the fights with great martial artists."

I said, "It won't work. You can't do that anymore. The people won't accept it. In a martial arts film today the fans demand that the actors really do it themselves."

He hit me with, "It's too much for you. You won't be able to pull it off." So, I gave him a little bit of each character, jumped around the room, talked in different voices, kicked at chairs and walls. He said, "OK! OK! But you absolutely can't play the girl's part!"

Kam Yuen was signed up to do the fight choreography and play one of the parts. We started auditioning fighters. I stepped up my workouts even more. We were on our way.

In movies you need doubles for everything, and the silent flute was going to see a lot of action—so I made three identical flutes about five feet long. That way they could be used as staffs as well. One was destroyed in battle, one I gave to the director, and one I still have.

At that time, Joe Lewis, the legendary competition karate fighter (four times world champion), was in the midst of a fling at acting. There was talk of using him to play Cord. An incredibly handsome man, he didn't like to risk having his face messed up. When full contact karate came in, he made a practice of

defeating most of his opponents in twenty seconds or
so. He never felt out an adversary, but simply charged
straight in with knockout kicks and punches, throwing
a sustained assault as brutal as was necessary to take
his man out, now! He once told me he always hurried
it up because he was eager to get on to the victory
party and meet some women.

When Joe retired from competition, he got his
head turned around for a while by the show-biz
wicked ways. It happens to most of us. He lost some
of his beauty and some of his sweetness, but he
straightened up and conquered the demons, as he
always has, and always will. He made a brief comeback
in competition at the amazing age of forty-one, knock-
ing some of the tough younger fighters on their back-
sides, before he slipped away again into the land of the
giants.

As it turned out, he did get to play Cord—in a
way. At the end of the production, Sandy decided we
needed to juice up the movie with a couple of extra
action sequences. Part of his one-hundred-ten percent
system. Jeff was unavailable, so Joe Lewis put on a
long-haired wig and filled in for him as Cord. It was a
terrifying experience to see that mass of muscle flying
through the air toward me at the speed of a freight
train.

Joe's ability to slip a punch is astounding. Once I
saw him take a fall, head first, and almost get his head
split open by a piece of steel that was sticking out
across his path. He turned a somersault in the air, just
clearing the steel, and landed in a crouch right under-
neath it. I asked him how was it he could move that
fast, and, in midair besides, without even having his
feet on the ground. Joe shrugged, and said, "Well, I've
slipped so many punches . . ."

Joe is a sweet guy when he's not breaking your
head, and we got along really well.

I was still having a hard time selling Jeff Cooper
to Sandy. I knew he was the right choice to play Cord.
We had alternated the roles of Teacher and Seeker in

real life for years, so it seemed natural to continue doing it on film, but Sandy wasn't buying it.

One day we all got together at Kam's school in a power meeting to see if it would gel. There were a lot of fighters around, showing their stuff. Jeff and I got into it. We started out sparring easily, with me trying out bits and pieces of the Monkey King style on him. Suddenly, things got serious, and when we stepped away we had drawn blood. Sandy was convinced. Hell, he was zapped. It was agreed. Jeff Cooper was Cord. I was everybody else.

Always the lone wolf, Jeff decided to look elsewhere for his final cram training, determined to develop his own very different style. Cord is supposed to be a mean, rough, renegade of a fighter, so Jeff worked out in a sort of kung-fu-outlaw-biker place for a while, doing heavy bag work and a lot of full contact. Then he discovered Mike Vendrell.

Mike Vendrell has no documented history of kung fu training in his background as far as I know. He has practiced the art since childhood with no discernible instructor. Mike had a fire that burned in him to be a part of this movie. I met Mike through Jeff. In the beginning our association was purely social, fueled mainly out of curiosity. He told me that he had an ambition to be a stuntman. He was a member of the Teamsters, so on my next movie, a motorcycle film shooting in Oklahoma called *Fast Charlie, the Moonbeam Rider,* I brought him along as my driver. I told him I would introduce him to the stuntmen, most of whom I knew pretty well from other films, and the rest would be up to him.

Throughout the movie I studied with Mike informally. His coaching was almost always in sparring. He would match his style with mine, work at my level of proficiency, then gradually lift me to higher levels, changing styles rapidly and talking all the while—coaxing, teasing, threatening, praising, probing, story telling, philosophizing.

Mike gave me two very strong lessons: one in

inventing my own animal forms and the other a powerful focusing exercise for specific development of chi strength.

Steve Carver, the director, turned out to be a real guy. He liked Mike and gave him his shot. Mike's first stunt was crashing a motorcycle into a hay bale. Never having been on a bike, the crashing part was easy for him; coming out of it in one piece was the hard part. He made it through and then proved himself useful in other ways. Mike is a doctor of sorts. I have seen him—more than once—make an injury disappear on the spot. There was a lot of call for that kind of thing on *Moonbeam Rider.*

He has healing hands and is adept at joint manipulation, reflexology, massage, and other curative therapies, such as a passive skeletal alignment similar to the "Alexander technique," and a "gong" therapy in which differently pitched massive bronze bells are placed around the subject's body and struck alternately in patterns and cycles designed to clear blockage and align the chi. The amazing thing about all this is that it works. If this is hard to believe, you've got Mike exactly; hard to believe! I have seen him receive the dim mak, or "touch of death," and survive it.

Mike got his stunt card on that picture and made it into *The Silent Flute.* He's now a stunt coordinator with many credits, including teaching kung fu to Arnold Schwarzenegger.

DEATHSPORT

After *Moonbeam Rider* I had a final contractual obligation with Roger Corman, before I could get back to *The Silent Flute*. I was supposed to do a sequel, of sorts, to *Death Race 2000*. It was to be a futuristic-sword-fighting-motorcycle picture. It turned out to be pretty much of a fiasco.

Relations were strained. Then, Nick Nicifor, the director/writer, quit the picture in the middle and left Roger's young and inexperienced apprentices to finish it.

Another big damper was thrown on things during this picture when I took a bad spill off a motorcycle and pulled a ligament in my right knee. The orthopedic surgeon told me it was a permanent injury. He also said I had to give it complete rest. I pointed out that I was in the middle of an action movie and had to be back on the bike that afternoon. He shot me up with cortisone and painkillers, gave me a brace, and I went back to work. But, how was I going to be able to do *The Silent Flute*?

When Kam found out about the injury, he took me to Leo Wang. Leo Wang is a wing chun Master. He is small and very strong and vital. He is able to imitate many styles and animals. I later took a class from him, only briefly, but the principles he taught me will always be with me.

Leo examined my knee and said, "Oh. Ligament. Very hard to heal. Sometimes never the same." That sounded a lot better than "permanent injury." He treated me with herbs and massage. I threw in DMSO (race horse medicine) and agni yoga or "actionism," as the New Age calls it—a form of restorative meditation. The knee started to get better right away, so I called up a beautiful girl I knew who also practiced the yoga, and we meditated together while she massaged me with the herbs. This treatment worked pretty well, and it certainly helped to pass the time.

The ligament eventually did heal completely, but it took over a year. I ended up doing *The Silent Flute* with the brace in place.

Our remaining problem with *The Silent Flute* was the director. We went around in circles about this. I was in favor of James Coburn. He knew more about *The Silent Flute* than anybody. He had the brains and the artistry, and he was eager to do it, but the idea of the actor turned director had not yet quite proven itself in Hollywood at that time. For various reasons a long list was whittled down to Richard Moore, an award-winning cinematographer who wanted to direct. He was eager, open-minded, technically proficient, to say the least, and willing to work cheap, being more or less financially independent.

Meanwhile, for reasons I could never divine, Sandy Howard thought it necessary to do a rewrite on the script. It seemed perfect to me as it was. Stanley Manne, a screenwriter with formidable credits, was brought in.

In my estimation, Stanley's main contributions were an argument between the Boatman and his wife (in the old legends the Boatman is the Buddha, and not likely to have a nagging wife, but it takes all kinds) and the Man in Oil (played by Eli Wallach), who is standing in a huge pot of oil, trying to dissolve his genitals to get rid of Desire.

THE FOURTH TRIAL

Heaven and Earth are ruthless.
Lao tzu

 We started filming in Israel late in 1977. We showed up in Tel Aviv in force. Kam had assembled a dozen or so martial artists. The crew was Israeli and British. The producer and director were American. We shot in locations with important historical and religious significance. I have always felt that this significance somehow managed to become a part of the picture.

As an example, there is a fortress which guards the pass between Tel Aviv and Jerusalem which dates back thousands of years. The pass was, at one time or another, controlled by many different factions of the various Holy Wars, sometimes for hundreds of years, sometimes for a day. This could be seen by the different architectural styles in which the fortress was built, strengthened, repaired and expanded: Phoenician, Sephardic, Persian, Turkish, Crusader, Egyptian, English.

At night in the courtyard of the castle, lit by a bonfire, we performed a fight to the death between the blind Master, armed with the silent flute, and eight rogues. Standing on the walls around us, Israeli soldiers appeared and disappeared quietly, armed and in uniform, watching for awhile and then going on back to their holy war. In the dust beneath us was the blood of three or four thousand years of defenders and aggressors.

David Carradine as Ah Sahm, the blind Master, in
Circle of Iron (The Silent Flute).
Photo by Eli Ben-Ari.
© 1978 Abco-Embassy Films.
All Rights Reserved.

The silent flute, the best one of them, broke during that fight.

In the story of *The Silent Flute,* the Seeker continually leaves his chosen path to follow his Master. He can always find the Master by following the sound of the meditation flute he plays. The flute is also the teacher's staff and his weapon. As Cord, the Seeker, follows his Master, he is led, seemingly by accident, through three trials. The three trials represent things within himself that he must overcome. The first is that beast that lives within us all. The second is death. The third is the pull of the "Earth Power" which makes the Seeker's spirit earthbound and his goals inadequate.

As he proceeds, the Seeker stumbles on a fourth trial, which is the most difficult of all. He has to learn, through great anguish, the ephemeral and unattainable nature of male-female love.

When Cord finally discovers the Book that contains the knowledge he seeks, he finds that the pages are all blank. (In the movie, they are mirrors.) Cord turns his back on the eternal luxury that is offered him and goes on, committed to an endless quest.

*If the sage
would guide
the people,
He must serve
with humility.
If he would lead
them, he must
follow behind.*
Lao tzu

LONE WOLF

With *The Silent Flute* in the can, I went on
with my life as a movie actor, studying the
arts less and less. Though I always kept up
my friendship with Sifu Kam Yuen, I gradually drifted away from the martial arts community.

Still, I couldn't really escape the art completely.

Kung Fu had gone into world-wide syndication
and was now more popular than ever. People everywhere wanted to talk to me. They all asked the same
old question: Do you really know karate? And a new
one: Are you ever going to make any more of them? I
started thinking about it.

It didn't seem like a bad idea. The *Star Trek* movies were going strong right then, and I could see certain parallels. The only hitch was, as time went on, I
wasn't at all sure I remembered how to do the character of Caine. Nevertheless, without really trying to, I
started to get an idea for a story, for something sort of
like *Son of Kung Fu*.

While I was thinking about it, I went to New
York to host *Saturday Night Live*. We did a skit where
Caine is walking through Harlem and goes into a hab-
erdashery for a drink of water. Eddie Murphy tries to
sell him some cool clothes, and Master Po talks to him
through a mirror. Then, in slow motion, he kicks the
store to pieces and dismembers a store window
dummy. Playing it for laughs, I felt absolutely free to

David Carradine in Circle of Iron (The Silent Flute).
Photo by Eli Ben-Ari.
© 1978 Abco-Embassy Films.

try anything. I discovered the character of Caine came back to me as though we'd never been apart.

Radames Pera, who had played little Grasshopper in the series, was grown up now, and living in New York. We went out to dinner together one night. There were helium-filled balloons dangling in the restaurant. We inhaled the helium and said lines from *Kung Fu* in chipmunk voices. Then we settled down and talked about the idea I had for the movie. It turned out Radames had an idea for a story very much like mine. We both thought the movie should be set in China. I thought it would be great if we could actually *shoot* the film there. I remembered Jim Weatherill saying how he longed to see a shot of Kwai Chang Caine playing his flute beside the Great Wall.

The next morning in the NBC cafeteria, with a helium hangover, I wrote the ideas down on a napkin.

When I got back to California, I talked to Warner Brothers about it, and after dragging their feet for a while, they decided to put together a script using our story.

All of a sudden, I was back in the game. I started working out seriously again and spent many hours, days and weeks with the writer, loaning him books and telling him stories, explaining my ideas for *Kung Fu, the Movie,* as we were calling it.

About this time, I ended the loneliness of a dead marriage (with the same woman with whom I had lost the key to Kam's kwoon on Mulholland Drive). I took up with Gail Jensen, a farmer's daughter who was to become my life-long partner and last wife. She told me that an old friend of hers, Steve Carver, was doing a Chuck Norris picture. I thought back to *Moonbeam Rider,* its director Steve Carver and thought, "Perfect!"

We went over to Orion Pictures and talked to Steve and Mike Metavoy (president of Orion), whom I knew from *Bound for Glory.* Mike said, "What do you think about doing a picture with Chuck Norris?" The film was called *Lone Wolf McQuade.*

I said, "When? Let's do it." A movie with Chuck

David Carradine in Lone Wolf McQuade.
© *1983 Orion Pictures Corporation.*
All Rights Reserved.

sounded like a sure way to find out if I still had the touch.

I started working out every morning with Rob Moses, one of Kam Yuen's former instructors. Rob was easily the most flexible martial artist I had ever seen, and he was up on all the same styles that had, by now, become my old friends. I worked out with Rob in the mornings, and in the afternoons I studied competition karate techniques with P.J. Lee.

I know very little about P.J. He was a competition karate fighter in Europe until an injury took him out of that rat race. When I met him, he was a partner in a shotoken school, and he was the head bouncer at a really rough nightclub in Hollywood. My brother Mike was a bouncer at the same club, and P.J.'s student, as well.

I thought it would help me when I came up against Chuck to know something about competition karate. It turned out to be not additive at all; but, simply, limiting. Rigorous, I'll say that for it, hard and fast, but the bouncers' techniques were actually more interesting—spontaneous, sudden, ingenious and obviously necessary for survival. Real.

P.J.'s teaching was the most strenuous I have ever had to endure. The sessions would begin with exhausting calisthenics, then proceed to practice on classic techniques, bag work, sparring and competition fighting combinations. All this at a breakneck pace.

I showed up on the El Paso set in great shape and plunged into work. Chuck carries several fighters with him, many of them left over from when he had a chain of Chuck Norris schools. I worked out with these fighters every day for three weeks, choreographing the fights. Steve Carver ran into me one afternoon and told me he'd heard I was doing some great stuff. He seemed surprised. I said, "Well, Steve, I didn't come to you completely unprepared." What with the years of performing in a weekly TV martial arts show, I'd done more of these fights than just about anyone else on earth. And, lucky me, relatively painlessly.

Classic confrontation between karate and kung fu in Lone
Wolf McQuade: *Chuck Norris, four times world champion,
plain, hard, solid stance; David Carradine, free and flowing
Northern Shaolin style.*

Chuck never came to our sessions. The first time I ever worked out with him was the day we started shooting the fight. He turned out to be very easy to work with. Smooth and totally professional. Well, it was to be expected. After all, he was the real thing.

Chuck, whose real name is Carlos, is a devout Christian. He doesn't smoke or drink, except for an occasional beer. He works out twice a day, morning and evening. He's a very pleasant and friendly man but kind of dull. However, if he doesn't get his workout one day, he can be almost too exciting to be around. Stay out of his way on those days, because he needs the outlet of his workout to take the steam out of him.

Chuck's brother, Aaron, works hand-in-hand with him in the movies. They couldn't be more different from one another. Aaron is big, almost fat, hard drinking, and a practical joker. He's a talented martial artist, though not as dedicated as Chuck.

Chuck and I had great fun in the movie's big fight scene. I had intended to use some of the karate combinations I'd learned from P.J., but, as it turned out, I ended up using my Northern Shaolin and tai Mantis stuff. The contrast in styles made the fight with Chuck a real classic. Maybe the best of all the ones I've had.

It took us four days to shoot that fight, and, by the end, we were so sore that we were hobbling around like little old men. My old ruined ligament was acting up, and Chuck had pulled a muscle in his groin, which made his famous flying, reverse-spinning heel kick very painful for him. Still, we both loved every minute of it.

There was a lot of bull in the media at that time about us not getting along. Nothing could be further from the truth. There was a big deal, supposedly, about who wins the fight in the movie, since there was a clause in my contract that said I could not be defeated in hand-to-hand combat with Chuck. This was an effort on the part of my people to protect my image.

In the end, the movie fight was never concluded. We switched to guns at a certain point, and then Chuck blew me up with a hand-grenade. Chuck's character actually took most of the punishment, as is his style in his pictures. He is always getting the hell beaten out of him and then coming back strong. Supposedly, the lawyers went to a screening of the rough cut with stop-watches. The longest I was down for was four seconds. Chuck was down for seven seconds, so it's pretty much a matter of interpretation about who won that fight.

The point was, as far as I was concerned, the fight looked great, and some of my best acting was when I was getting hit. What with my face going out of shape as it snapped around and the spray of sweat, it was hard for *me* to believe Chuck wasn't really connecting. It looked like a real prize fight. I've never seen anything like it in a movie before. I wouldn't have cut that footage out for the world.

The whole thing, including the idea that there was a lawsuit, was a publicity stunt to sell tickets. It worked pretty well. *Lone Wolf* was, by a huge margin, the most successful Chuck Norris picture to date. And, while the lawyers and publicists were fighting it out, Chuck and I were laying back, having a beer together. He liked Pearl; I preferred Lone Star.

It was also rumored that Chuck broke my nose or that I broke his. Sorry to disappoint everybody, but we never touched each other. We were perfect gentlemen. My nose has been broken four times, but never by Chuck Norris.

I have great respect for Chuck, and he for me. Chuck says I'm about as good a martial artist as he is an actor.

SWORD
AND SORCERY

Warner Brothers was bogging down on *Kung Fu, the Movie,* so I looked around for some other way to make use of my renewed interest in martial arts. My old friend Roger Corman came up with it. He sent me the script of *Cain of Dark Planet,* a sword-fighting picture that takes place on another planet. It was to be shot in Argentina. It was essentially a remake of *Yojimbo,* the samurai movie by the great Japanese director, Akira Kurosawa. I called up Roger and told him I loved the script; but what about the *Yojimbo* factor. Roger said, "Yes, it is rather like *Yojimbo.*"

I said, "It's not like *Yojimbo.* It is *Yojimbo.*"

Roger said, "Let me tell you a story. When *Fist Full of Dollars* opened in Tokyo, Kurosawa's friends called him up and said 'You must see this picture.'

"Kurosawa replied, 'Yes, I understand it's rather like *Yojimbo.*'

" 'No, it's not like *Yojimbo;* it is *Yojimbo.* You have to sue these people.'

" 'I can't sue them,' he responded.

"'Why not?'

" 'Because,' Kurosawa confessed, '*Yojimbo* is Dashiel Hammet's *Red Harvest.*' "

I went for it.

The title was eventually changed to *The Warrior and the Sorceress,* which was odd since there was no

David Carradine in The Warrior and the Sorceress.
© *1984 Concorde-New Horizons Corp.*

sorceress in it, only a priestess. Roger said market research had told him the new title would sell more tickets.

When I arrived in Argentina for filming, I was informed that one Anthony de Longis was to play the bad guy and choreograph the swordplay. I had a grudge with Tony that dated back to *The Silent Flute*. I asked, "If I kill someone over a blood feud in Argentina, what will happen to me?"

I was told: "In Argentina, no problem."

As it turned out, Tony and I became friends, and I had to abandon my grudge.

Three days into the shoot, I broke my right hand in five places, so the picture had, for me, the added advantage of teaching me how to use a sword with my left hand.

For some reason, everybody in Argentina seemed to want to fight me. I was forced to answer a number of challenges. They were all punks, so the situations were never actually life-threatening, even with a broken hand. It never took more than a couple of moves or so to dispose of the threats. I didn't hurt these pilgrims, just neutralized them, maybe humbled them a little. One of the convenient things about martial arts mastery is that really dangerous fighters rarely feel they have to prove it to you. At any rate, all the fighting incidents seemed to strengthen my image in Argentina, and, in between challenges, this great, left-handed sword-fighting picture got made.

Since the story was supposed to take place on another planet, we thought the sword play should look like nothing anyone had ever seen before, so, between us, Tony and I worked out a special style. It was a combination of classical French fencing, tae kwon do, kung fu, Philippine stick fighting and some stuff we made up ourselves.

The movie went well, though it never played much in theaters due to a decision by the director, who costumed the priestess in a topless outfit. Everywhere you look there was this bare-breasted woman.

Since the picture's primary appeal was to kids, censorship dictated that it would never really reach its audience. It has, however, become something of a hit on
cassette.

If you get a chance, by all means take a look at it,
if not for the exotic bare-breasted priestess then for the
exotic left-handed sword play. I kill fifty-two people in
it and, each time, use a slightly different, esoteric blade
technique.

DAVID AS
THE TEACHER

Back in California, Sifu had come up with some tasks for me. He wanted me to write this book, and he wanted to make a video cassette instructing people in the art of kung fu. Actually, he wanted two cassettes: one on kung fu and one on t'ai chi. He wanted me to be the instructor, so he introduced me to his partners, who knew a lot about martial arts and nothing about making movies. They had done one thing, however, that gave me faith in them. They had hired Kent Wakeford to photograph it. Kent did the photography for Martin Scorsese's *Mean Streets* and he is one of the best, in my book.

In the kung fu video, I teach, along with Kam, a class with stretches, stances, kicking and punching, breathing techniques and combination exercises (the first four). There are also demonstrations of five of the basic Animal styles. At the end of the tape, I demonstrate combination exercises five through eight, though I don't teach them. After all, only so much can be assimilated at one time. Later, we will make a more advanced video which will present exercises five through eight and the Law Horn form.

The t'ai chi video begins with a remarkable demonstration of chi strength by Sifu. Then, we teach a class together and give step-by-step instruction in the

David Carradine instructing a student in the
Northern Praying Mantis technique.

t'ai chi form. The form is demonstrated twice by Kam and once by myself.

The two videos are very different in their natures and applications. The kung fu tape is vigorous, sometimes strenuous, potentially challenging. The t'ai chi tape is soft and flowing, calming but still challenging. Both of them are dynamic and graceful. One for men and one for women, if you will, but, we hope that the public will end up crossing over the lines, from hard to soft, from the yin to the yang.

Kam and I felt that there is a real need for these films, if only to offer an alternative to the glut of mindless exercise tapes that are on the market. Though there is no way a person can become a kung fu expert by watching a video, the tapes are excellent introductions to the art. Hopefully, they will move the seeker to find a live teacher and continue studying.

One final thing about the tapes: they are the only workout videos of any kind that I've seen that are worth just sitting and watching. You don't actually have to do the exercises. The tapes are interesting and entertaining, because the knowledge contained in the words which accompany the exercises are informative, instructive and fulfilling in themselves.

The videos are constructed to be valuable to students of all levels. Even a Master can find some kernel of new knowledge in them.

15

GRASSHOPPER LIVES

*A Journey of a
thousand miles
Starts under
one's feet.*
Lao tzu

It was finally decided to film *Kung Fu, the Movie* as a movie for TV. I thought this was a marketing error, myself. There is a lot more money to be made in a blockbuster movie. A TV show, however, would reach more people, and TV was where Kwai Chang Caine's fans were, so I said yes.

The change to TV meant we couldn't film in China and required an extensive rewrite and a delay. We also lost Radames Pera. The studio, in its infinite wisdom, had selected Bruce Lee's son, Brandon, to play Caine's son. Radames and I didn't get credit for our original story, and they wouldn't let me have Jim Weatherill or Herman Miller. Jerry Thorpe, Alex Beaton, Chuck Arnold and Richard Rawling were unavailable. You can't always get what you want.

While I was waiting for the rewrite, I went about my life and continued with the finishing touches for the instructional videos. They seemed to need some more footage, so I volunteered to pay for some extra shooting. The editing was not going well, and the music wasn't good enough, so I brought in David Kern, whom I had trained myself (though he has since far surpassed my abilities in that area). The music problem was solved by giving the job to my wife, known in the field as Gail Jensen, a singer, songwriter and record producer of great ability and some note.

With the videos resolved and in the works, I went off to the Philippines to film *Behind Enemy Lines,* later changed to *P.O.W. the Escape.* I had to do the final pre-production on *Kung Fu, the Movie* by remote control, from Manila. However, I felt secure about doing it this way since Richard Lang was the director of the film, and he was the person I most trusted with the material, given that Jerry Thorpe was unavailable.

There was some good kung fu fighting in *P.O.W.,* so I arrived at Warner Brothers in a high state of training. Three days into the shoot, I broke my hand again. I expected Richard Lang to be devastated by that news, but he merely looked at my hand and said, "That should make it more interesting." Richard loves a challenge.

The filming of *Kung Fu, the Movie* was just like old times. Lots of the old boys were on hand: Keye Luke, of course, Benson Fong, Roy Jensen, Kam Yuen, Mako, Mike Vendrell, Alan Fama, Jim Spahn. There were some great new people: Kerry Kean, Luke Askew, Bill Lucking, Martin Landau. For extra spice, my oldest daughter, Calista, had a part. We knocked out an excellent show, and, as Richard Lang proudly announced at the end of the last day of shooting, we did it without a single camera trick.

After the show was aired, there was talk of doing a new series—a modernized version of *Kung Fu* with Brandon and me playing Caine's great and great, great grandsons. It was to be produced by the team that had been responsible for *The Dukes of Hazzard.* I had visions of kung fu car crashes and decided to pass.

16

THE TWELVE LESSONS

The sage is guided by what he feels and not by what he sees. The hard and strong will fall. The soft and weak will overcome. The truth often sounds paradoxical.
Lao tzu

The Master teaches the Seeker. There are twelve lessons, as far as I have been able to determine. Each of them is an accepted truth in Taoist, Buddhist or Hindu teachings. Or Norse, or Native American, for that matter.

1. Follow the heart.

2. There are no secrets.

3. Laugh at the cleverness of the beast and the beast will defeat itself.

4. Death is nothing to one who does not fear death.

5. Love, in the pain of its loss, is finally gained, for the first time.

6. You, yourself, are your only teacher.

7. Kindness is cruelty, cruelty is kindness.

8. Stop for charity, no matter what the cost, and there will be benefit instead of cost. It does not matter for whom.

9. It has all happened before. Everyone and no one has been here before, and no matter how obscure it may seem to you, "the universe is . . . unfolding as it should," or more precisely, as it cannot help but do.

10. There are no prizes worth having.

11. The ultimate quest has no ending, and that fact is what gives the quest its ultimate value.

12. Tie two birds together and they *can* fly, if they become One.

The whole thing is pretty loose and haphazard. It barely holds water; however, "barely" is just enough. Once you get these down, there's a whole new set of them down the next path. Lesson #11, remember? Don't expect to find an end to it, there isn't one.

The surprising thing that I discovered after the completion of *The Silent Flute,* the thing it taught me, aside from the realization that I still had an enormous amount to learn, and that I definitely am not Bruce Lee, was that the true nature of kung fu is not in Bruce's story, or in any other story. The essence still remains largely untold. Only one small piece of the mystery is revealed, as it turns out.

A new project is now in preparation which will attempt, once again, to achieve this goal. However, I have come to believe that no story will ever encompass the whole truth. I believe that as these truths are revealed, the essence actually changes, remaining forever out of reach. Still, it's important to keep trying. I suppose it's good karma, and every piece of the puzzle clarifies some aspect of the mystery.

BOOK TWO

THE ANCIENT
WISDOM

THE
ESSENCE

Looking straight into the heart and acting thence is the root; the wealth is a by-product.
Tseng

The truly great man dwells on what is real and not what is on the surface. On the fruit and not the flower.
Lao tzu

Kung fu is an ancient fitness program through which humankind realizes its full potential through better understanding, learning to set higher limits and standards, transcending rigid and false values and achieving harmony with the laws of nature and the universe. Kung fu is a training with a useful purpose, and leads to the learning of refined skills which will remain with the student for a lifetime, and, perhaps, even longer.

The drills of Shaolin kung fu serve to put us in touch mentally with our physical selves, so that we no longer remain strangers to our own bodies. One finds true strength and inner peace within when mind and body work as one. Conflict arises when the mind tries to dominate and push the body beyond its limits. How is one expected to be able to get along with others and with nature if one has lost the ability to be in harmony with oneself? The mind that works against the body creates a continual state of conflict and struggle.

The purpose of any study program or every self-determination of any kind is, ultimately, to improve the quality of existence. Any other value is secondary to this primary goal: benefit. Peace and tranquility benefit. Tension and strain do not. Initially, the tranquil student may not achieve as much, or progress as fast as one who pushes and drives the body with mind and ego; but, in the long run, the student who maintains inner calm and stresses mind and body synchronization in his training will go far beyond the level which could ever be achieved by one who is forever straining and fighting to achieve a successful workout or other goals in life—one to whom every training session is a test, and completion of every task the end in itself.

"No pain, no gain" is the modern day obsession in certain physical training and a common litany perpetuated by trainers who profess more often than not to be omnipotent gurus. Not to say that this attitude will not produce certain impressive results, but, for the purposes of this manual, and for long-term gains, good health and longevity, let's just say that nothing beats feeling good.

Exercise that is torture, or so dull and monotonous that loud music must be played and orders shouted, will not achieve for us the enlightenment we desire.

The basic difference between the study of martial arts, and other exercise programs, such as weight training or aerobics, is that with these other disciplines you will have learned all there is to know after a few short weeks. Beyond that it is simply a matter of repetition. Kung fu, on the other hand, continues to teach the body and the mind throughout life, and further establishes and strengthens the communication link between the two.

Thought controls the body's action and when thought is distracted, the body becomes a mindless robot—as when it is subjected by outside forces to bouncing up and down and waving arms and legs in space for no purpose other than exercise.

In the study of kung fu, every movement has a function beyond itself and an application to the real world we live in. Moreover, every movement contains within it a metaphor to lead the disciple toward the comprehension of the wisdom of the ages.

Whether kung fu remains definable as a martial art at all with such a philosophy is not important in the end. We do not call kung fu a martial art, or a religion, or a philosophy. We call it a *Way of Life*.

Kung fu can be applied to every situation in life. It is whatever you want it to be. You are in control of yourself and your situation when you accept kung fu as such.

All the defensive and offensive techniques can be mastered in a short period of time without great difficulty. A bright student can become adept at the physical aspects of kung fu in a year or two. I have seen it happen.

The *purpose* of kung fu, however, is not so easily revealed. A lifetime of devotion may not unfold the basic cosmic truths of which the movements of kung fu are a mere metaphorical hint. The important thing is to devote oneself to it anyway. The rewards to be found along the way are more than enough to make the journey worthwhile.

Still, by far the best way is to perform the tasks without regard to the rewards. This is the purest kind of devotion, and will ultimately take the seeker closer to his goal.

A slow student requires more devotion, and, if he can find that dedication within himself, he has more chance of reaching the truth than a quicker pupil who accepts the knowledge casually. Devotion is the key, the question, and perhaps a large part of the answer, as well.

Desire, determination, perseverance and practice are the keys to success in kung fu. Size and sex don't matter. Almost anyone can learn and perform these moves, and the mind and spirit will progress side by side with the body. Women do well in the Northern systems because they naturally excel in the grace, acrobatics and balletic moves found in these styles. Children are clean slates. They can be taught like puppies. They benefit greatly from the discipline, coordination, speed, mental coordination and confidence they develop—little realizing the subtler inner progress they are undergoing at the same time.

Looking for a *way* among the questions. Attempting, through discipline and practice, to discover a higher plane of life on Earth. One without fear or anger, with everything in balance and, at the same time, deliciously exciting. All leading to a state which is totally above and outside previous experience.

This is what kung fu is about.

One other style of learning which I must mention is that of the Outlaw. There is no predicting this seeker's progress. It might be meteoric or catastrophic. Usually this individual evolves through a process something like mutation: dangerous, unpredictable, sometimes brilliant, innovative, destructive or disruptive: who knows? This style cannot really be affected or assimilated. It is built into the person to begin with. *You* know who you are. It's what I am.

Kung fu today is enjoying an immense popularity around the world. This is at least partly due to the influence of the television program *Kung Fu,* which characterizes martial arts as an ultimate problem solver, something to resort to when all else has failed. In the *Kung Fu* TV series (now seen in seventy-one different markets world-wide), unlike the genre movies on the subject, the characters deal philosophically with confrontations with evil, resorting to physical violence only in absolute extremity, and even then with great restraint.

This attitude is inherent to kung fu artists of most styles. It can put them physically, mentally and spiritually above their adversaries and difficulties. It is this very attitude that appeals so strongly to people in today's world; for we live in a time when there is little in which to put our faith and trust except our belief in powers beyond ourselves, and beyond the temporal and materialistic values of the society in which we live.

THE HISTORY

 There is no way the philosophy of kung fu can be understood without some knowledge of its history. Kung fu came into being in the 6th century A.D. when Bodhidharma, a wandering monk travelling through northern China, came across a Taoist temple in the Shangshon mountains. Known as the Shaolin monastery, the temple was full of spiritually and mentally superior monks whose bodies were frail. (The story is that they were so weak they would fall asleep during their lessons.) Bodhidharma taught the monks a Hindu discipline—one that he had modified. The discipline was a form of active meditation, a holy dance that strengthened the body while it provided a key to the knowledge that was contained in Hindu philosophy.

Bodhidharma also expanded the monks' knowledge about the Hindu prophet Buddha. Born in 560 B.C., Buddha's real name was Gautama Siddhartha. He became a teacher and moralist who proposed a way of life based on the simple goal of "usefulness." He sat down beneath the Bodhi Tree (*bodhi* translates as illumination), and, when he rose again, he was enlightened.

These three things—Bodhidharma's discipline, the related Hindu philosophy, and Buddhist ideas—mingled with Taoist thought to become kung fu. Literally, kung fu means "to know what to do."

Portrait of Bodhidharma, drawn by Li Kuchan.
From Shaolin Kung Fu *by Ying Zi and Weng Yi.*

Thirty years before Bodhidharma left India for China, a monk named Batua made the same pilgrimage. Batua was very well-received by the emperor, who built the Shaolin temple for Batua to teach his wisdom. Batua filled the temple with Taoist monks, and he taught Buddha to them. His teachings became known as *Old Chinese Buddhism*. When Bodhidharma arrived and presented himself to the emperor, he was not as well-received. The old emperor had died in the intervening thirty years, and the new emperor did not think that Bodhidharma could do very much, because Bodhidharma wasn't a great talker.

Bodhidharma left the emperor and headed for Shangshon Mountain and the Shaolin temple. On the way, he crossed the Yangtze River by floating, or so legend has it, on a little stick with five leaves. He spent the subsequent nine years "facing the wall" in a state of meditation in a cave on Shangshon Mountain. Eventually, he took a disciple. According to the story, the disciple, after several years of vain supplication, cut off his own arm to illustrate his sincerity and devotion to Bodhidharma.

While Bodhidharma was sitting "facing the wall," he had problems with his muscle tone. He also had to contend with wild animals and snakes. As a solution to these problems, making use of the disciplines he had learned in India, he developed the eighteen forms of ahrat. These techniques mingled with hudi and juedi—ancient Chinese survival systems which existed long before the Shaolin—to become the true beginning of kung fu. Years later, six of the eighteen ahrat movements were lost. In the next century, the lost movements were reconstructed through meditation, divination and improvisation. These eighteen moves comprise the basis for the Law Horn system. The Law Horn is traditionally taught as the most ancient of forms, although the ahrat, which was probably not even intended as a formal system, predates the Law Horn. Today, there are one hundred and thirty-six

The entrance gate of the Shaolin Monastery,
Shangshon Mountain, China.
From Shaolin Kung Fu *by Ying Zi and Weng Yi.*

movements, or forms, in the Law Horn system, about eighteen of which use weapons.

Bodhidharma also started what was called *New Buddhism* which was more ascetic than the Batua variety of Buddhism. It stressed fasting and meditation and included Bodhidharma's five commandments against killing, robbery, obscenity, telling lies and drinking wine. Eating flesh was considered unwise, though there was no specific commandment against it. Silence was also highly prized and recommended. Centuries later, the commandments were broken and discarded when the emperor gave the monks meat to eat and wine to drink. This was called "The Changes of the Sixth Ancestor."

Shaolin warriors once led a rebellion of the Ming faction against the Ching dynasty. A new system of kung fu was evolved for this purpose. The system was called hungar. It made use of empty hands and common tools for weapons so as to allow apparently unarmed peasants to infiltrate among the emperor's soldiers and then suddenly attack and destroy them. The hungar system stance is incredibly wide and solid, more than any other form in the martial arts. The feet do not move, but rather wave back and forth. If there are any kicks at all they are low, with the power coming out of the earth. The system uses the hands: reaching, grabbing, punching. One of the styles within the hungar system was the Tiger Crane form which made use of the Long Finger style. (A usual stance in this style includes a hard hand with a single finger extended, as a symbol of the beak of the crane.) It was said about this style, "If every Ming will lift one finger, we will defeat the Ching."

In truth, no revolution ever had much success against the Imperial Chinese governments of antiquity. The dynasties all eventually fell through inner collapse. When the Ming revolution failed, one of the Shaolin masters, who had led and trained the rebels, fled to Okinawa. He attempted to enlist an army to try his cause again. When he was unsuccessful in doing this, he remained in Okinawa and taught. It is thought by some that his teachings travelled up the island chain to Japan and became karate.

As the influence of Shaolin philosophy and training spread, carrying Tao, Buddha and martial arts throughout the Far East, every style of Asian martial arts came to be based on some form of Chinese kung fu. Perhaps one of the newest and crudest of these is Japanese karate.

Much has been made of the difference between kung fu and karate. Actually, since all systems and styles are contained somewhere in kung fu, the basic truths are the same. The only real difference is that karate is an incomplete form of kung fu. In karate, and the other derivatives, the most "effective" or "useful" ideas are taught. Kung fu tries to make of itself a complete art in which *everything* is finally known, regardless of its "usefulness." The limitation in karate stems, at least in part, from its association with Japanese-style Buddhism, which ignores or forgets the Chinese Taoist principles and replaces them with the specific, and generally radical, ideas peculiar to the Japanese culture, i.e. Zen. Much could be said about the subject of Zen, but we are interested here in kung fu, so best look elsewhere for that.

THE
ONE THING

The great Tao
flows everywhere.
It fulfills its
purpose silently
and makes no
claim.
It does not show
greatness,
And is therefore
truly great.
Lao tzu

Complete, all
embracing, the
whole.
These numes
are different,
but the
reality sought
in them is
the same:
The One Thing.
Chuang-tzu

Virtually all Chinese thought originates from two basic sets of teaching: *Taoism,* a spontaneous, profound awareness of the true nature of things, expressed in mystical, poetic terms, and *Confucianism,* a pragmatic, practical set of moral standards and social etiquette. The two teachings are the opposite poles of Chinese thought. Confucianism deals with worldly affairs and physical reality while Taoism deals with spiritual transcendence and abstract philosophy. In China, a sage has to deal with both these concepts simultaneously. He has to be a poet-philosopher and a man of action.

Confucianism comes from the sage and teacher K'ung Fu-tzu, or Confucius, who lived during the 5th-6th century B.C. He established a set of rules and ethics for the maintenance of the family unit and the social order and for the preservation of traditions. Confucius' emphasis was on the practical, on how man should live his life. His wisdom is detailed in the *Wu Ching* (which includes the *I Ching*) and *Ssu Shu* (which includes the *Analects*).

Taoism originated with Lao tzu, a teacher who was, according to legend, an older contemporary of Confucius. His name means "the old master." His writings, in a book called *Tao Te Ching,* and the work of Chuang-tzu are the basic works of Taoism. *Tao Te Ching* literally means *changes in the way.* The book is, perhaps, the most beautiful and profound work of poetry and philosophy in any language. The way it came to be written was that Lao tzu, who was the sage and advisor of the emperor, decided one day to end his public life and walk on in search of *the Tao,* which is translated as *the Way* but is understood to be indefinable. *The Tao* is something like the universal, the main cosmic order of nature, but, even to say this is, already, to misspeak.

When Lao tzu, in his search for *the Tao,* came to the Great Wall of China, the guard at the gate recognized him and refused to allow him to pass unless he wrote his wisdom down first. Lao tzu sat down by the wall and, in a few hours, completed the *Tao Te Ching.* He left his words with the guard and crossed into Manchuria. He was never seen or heard from again.

Apparently, Lao tzu and Confucius taught each other their separate wisdoms. In China, both disciplines were taught to the people. Confucius was taught to young people to give them a foundation for proper behavior in society. *The Tao* was practiced by older people to maintain their flexibility and spontaneity and to infuse them with the necessary cosmic wisdom to prepare them for death and rebirth.

The Hindu teachings of Buddha came to China, from India, in the 5th century A.D. The teachings mingled with both Confucianism and Taoism to produce Neo-Confucianism, which was elaborated by a great sage named Chu H'si. Neo-Confucianism tried to move Confucianism towards Taoist thought, to make it more abstract and other-worldly, just as Neo-Taoism tried to move Taoism somewhat closer to the practical, worldly teachings of Confucianism.

The universal symbol of all Eastern religions, including Taoism, Confucianism and, later, Buddhism, is *t'ai c'hi t'u,* also called *the symbol of the ultimate supreme.* It is better known as the yin-yang. The symbol of two fish—one dark with a light eye and one light with a dark eye—chasing each other around in a circle is a metaphor for the active and passive forces in the universe. There is the dark, passive, female yin and the bright, active, male yang. These two forces swirl about and through each other, changing constantly. One becomes the other, and both always contain the seed of the other within (i.e., as the eye of the fish in the image).

The symbol has the same meaning as the other great religious symbols of the world: the Cross, the Madonna and Child, the Crescent and Star, the Star of David, the Sun and Moon. Since people throughout time have embraced the principle of yin-yang, though they have used different forms to do so, these various symbols may, in some real sense, comprise a true picture of the nature of all things.

Like the Eastern philosophies, kung fu is largely based on an extension of the concept of yin-yang. Indeed, the yin-yang is sometimes referred to as the symbol of martial arts. Actually, it is the symbol for everything. The yin-yang is also called a symbol of duality. However, this simplifies the truth. What the symbol really demonstrates is that duality is an illusion, that two sides of the same face add up to one face.

The notion that everything can be divided into two categories—one good, one evil—is what creates prejudice. Indeed, strict ethics is pure prejudice if the ethics judge every action in advance. In truth, actions cannot be labelled right or wrong. Everything is an experiment and each event yields some knowledge. All propositions and suppositions are true in some sense, false in some sense, and meaningless in some sense. (If this makes no sense to you, keep trying.)

The point is that it is the very perception of the world as full of opposites that creates opposites. The perceiving eye is partially responsible for what is seen. Thus, in a certain way, laws cause crime; capitalism causes socialism; good causes evil. The only way out of this rat race is to get past the whole concept of duality.

There is another form of the yin-yang, which I saw once as a Sufi symbol, but which probably can be found in other sects. This symbol looks like the yin-yang, but it has three, rather than two, elements swirling about in a circle. The suggestion, then, is that there are three things: this, that and the other thing.

In Taoist thinking, non-volitional living (acting by not-acting) is perceived to be the purest form of existence. They call this philosophy *wu wei*. In it, the subject-object concept is eliminated, as are the ideas of opposites or opponents. The perceiving eye and the sunset are the same thing. Without hope, there can be no despair. Without Heaven, no Hell.

It is difficult to embrace this philosophy whole-heartedly while living on this planet, but Taoists say it can be done. To my mind, the theory of relativity is a more workable alternative. Here, with the notion that the experiment and the experimenter affect each other, we can see that there are no absolutes, that all things are relative.

We can see what is *is*. Don't judge it. *Be* it.

Don't confuse the map with the territory. The map is not colored purple because the land is purple, it's a code. Einstein said that the difference between the concept and the word for it is not like the difference between beef and beef broth; it's like the difference between your overcoat and the ticket the hat-check girl gives you.

Science has always been obsessed with categories. It is actually not possible to talk about the cosmos itself, only about how we perceive the cosmos. Even then, we have to describe the cosmos in a code. Which is to say we have to use language, essentially a symbol for what we are talking about. To a great extent, we have made up the answers we have about the cosmos. The order that the scientist insists on is projected on to reality by the scientist's instruments.

There is no permanent reality except the reality of change. Permanence is an illusion of the senses. All things carry with them their opposites. Death is potential in life. Freedom and oppression go together, just as creation and destruction do. Being and non-being are part of every whole, therefore, the only possible real state is the transitional one of becoming.

In the darkness is the light. In strength is the softness. In the question is the answer. It is all one thing. Here is the enormous simplicity and complexity of the yin-yang metaphor. It is a great lesson and a difficult lesson, small and easy once it is learned.

Until it is learned, the illusion of duality is all we have. It is this concept of opposites, which is part of the illusion of duality, that causes problems. To make the puzzle complete and, therefore, no longer a puzzle, we need techniques.

The primary technique is *choice*. It begins to provide a solution to the positive-negative problem. Choose the positive to begin with and most of the rest will follow. Choose courage instead of fear. Choose success instead of failure. Choose harmony not conflict. Choose solutions not problems. Choose love not hate. Choose life instead of death. (If it is all one thing, anyway, why concentrate on the negative values at all?)

In discovering the positive side of certain questions, you automatically identify the negative. If you discard the negative, you are left with the entire positive truth. As an example, take the concept of good and evil. Face the evil and discard it. Turn to face what is left and you will find the good—infinite and complete. Good is all, and it was discovered by applying the spurious concept of yin and yang. Still, in practice, the moment that complete joy or despair is achieved, it will begin immediately to become its opposite. Count on it. Know it, and there is some chance of controlling it. A spiral upward is preferable to an endlessly repeated cycle. It is better to have someplace to fall from than someplace to fall to. In this high-flying quest, a parachute is preferable to an anchor.

A martial artist of my acquaintance once told me his Sensei (Japanese martial arts teacher) had told him never to trust anyone, including his Sensei. I replied, "And you trusted him when he told you that?"

The martial artist stumbled away, his neat system in jeopardy, and his mind reeling with new and confusing possibilities—the proper state for such a seeker.

SPIRITUALITY

*The Tao is an
empty vessel;
It is used but
never filled.*

*Heaven's net
casts wide.
Though its
meshes are
coarse,
nothing slips
through.*
Lao tzu

 Any in-depth discussion of kung fu philosophy will have to deal with spirituality, which can come perilously close to religion. All the scientific, religious and mystical systems of the world embrace the concept of a supreme power which governs the universe according to certain immutable laws. The path is to discover, affirm and understand the truths surrounding this one great Truth. *The Way* is to bring our world into harmony with the various truths we discover.

In the physical sciences, phenomena are observed and explanations are arrived at through experimentation and interpretation. In religion and mystic philosophy, the certainty of the theory is accepted, and it is the phenomena which are interpreted in accordance with the theory. This method of exploration requires *faith*. It is used when dealing with concepts which we cannot verify with our senses. Efforts to apply Einstein's theory of relativity are a perfect example of this; evidence is reinterpreted to prove the accepted theory. The truth is that scientists do a lot of this, but they don't like to admit it.

The application of this tool, faith, is what defines an experience as spiritual. Faith, when it is used in other areas, is called belief or instinct or inspiration. It is also mixed up intimately with chance and luck.

The true nature of what is spiritual and what is merely nonsense is hard to agree upon. A precise line cannot be drawn between faith, superstition and science. About all we can say without argument is that there is a larger reality which is beyond our comprehension. We don't have a name for it, but we know it exists. In practice, we find ourselves breaking through, at times, to an expanded reality in which we are able to perceive a whole new set of mysteries which were formerly invisible to us. Then, we discover the limitations of this new awareness and must break through yet again. This process is, as far as I have been able to discern, endless.

Ultimately, no amount of study will lead us to the whole truth. Even if we work continually for a lifetime, we will never come to the end of our explorations about Truth. This is where faith comes in. We accept the truth of theories we cannot prove and, in that way, perceive the whole picture, though its complete structure is beyond our understanding.

This method of exploring is not available to the cynic.

There is an old story about faith and cynicism. Two prospectors were sitting in a saloon up in Alaska. They were drinking and talking and the subject of God came up. "I don't believe in God," one of the prospectors said.

"You don't? Well, that's really unusual up here. Why not?" said the other one.

"Well, I used to, but I gave it up. You see, one time I was out there on the tundra, and there was this awful blizzard, and I got lost and was sure I was going to freeze to death. So, I got down on my knees and prayed to God to save me and absolutely nothing happened."

"Well, you damn fool," said the other prospector, "how can you say that? You're here, aren't you? You must have got out."

"Sure, I got out. But it wasn't God that did it.

Some damn Eskimo came along and showed me the way back to town."

Faith, hope and belief are valuable tools without which we cannot pursue the infinite. When these things become rigid in religious or ritualistic practices, they no longer serve that purpose. Faith is powerful, but only when accompanied by enlightenment. Faith can move mountains. Blind faith can plunge us into folly. So faith must be used carefully, like garlic.

Or, as an alternative method to dealing with faith, you can remember that cynicism is the first religion. It is the means by which to discover all else, since cynicism implies skepticism. Skepticism results in examination, and examination leads to understanding.

5

If the root be in
confusion,
nothing will be
well governed.
Confucius

I put on my
trousers one leg
at a time.
And I don't pull
the corn up by
its stalks
To make it grow.
old Taoist
saying

STYLE

Style is very important. More important is to
have no style, which, in an educated person,
is to have all styles.

Style is not a pattern to be repeated. It is
a puzzle. The idea is to embrace the style and then to
overcome it. Only in this way can we progress to new
levels of learning. Once every piece of the puzzle is in
its proper place, it is no longer a puzzle. It is a picture,
an image which then has to be examined until it is
understood. Then it becomes an actual thing—a tiny
piece of the true shape of the universe which one can
hold in one's hand.

The majority of instructors usually feel their own
style is the best. The important thing is to feel comfortable and enthusiastic with your chosen style. I have
studied several of the major styles in the martial arts,
but prefer the Northern styles of kung fu, which stress
long, flowing movements with both the hands and the
feet.

It is my opinion that the Northern styles, more
than any others, develop the total individual. Expan-
sive movements and stretches; free-flowing leg, arm
and body techniques, with especially high extensions
and elevated jumps; low floor moves, long reaches;
acrobatic flights. All of these are included in the
Northern system. Imagine the same techniques applied

Kam Yuen demonstrating his form.

to the mind and the spirit, and you have an idea of the extent of what can be found here.

Still, there is no one style that is best for everyone. When you hear of one style beating another in a contest, that does not mean that is the best style for you. For instance, in one tournament Thai kick boxers were victorious over Southern kung fu stylists from a Hong Kong school. It appears that the Thai style is superior to the one taught in that particular Hong Kong school; however, if you look deeper, you may understand why kickboxing, even though victorious in this situation, may not be the best choice for most people.

These Thai fighters were professionals who trained all day every day. They allowed themselves to become human punching bags to toughen their bodies to withstand the blows of their opponents. This may be effective, but not very enjoyable to most people, and certainly is not healthy practice. The challengers from Hong Kong were not professionals, and did not subject their bodies to daily physical beatings for the purpose of toughening themselves for combat.

It should also be noted that the equipment used included boxing gloves. This put the Hong Kong school at a disadvantage, as all open-handed, long finger, and grasping techniques could not be used. The use of gloves also diminished the power of the punches. The rule against techniques below the belt prohibited the use of leg sweeps and knee and leg kicks, some of the most effective techniques there are.

The Hong Kong school of Southern style kung fu was at a further disadvantage against the kickboxers. Their concentration on hand techniques for close-in fighting put them at a disadvantage in an open arena (such as a boxing ring) against the longer reaching leg techniques of kickboxers, Northern kung fu practitioners and Korean stylists.

These differences in approaches and rules always make formal contests between different disciplines inconclusive. The only way to arrive at a definite conclusion would be a real conflict, without rules, between champions. Still, this would only demonstrate the effectiveness of the discipline in battle—not its suitability for you in your life.

Underlying, sometimes indiscernible, circumstances are important in comparing styles. Moreover, consideration must be given to the quality of life which results from the study. Happiness and well-being are what this manual is intended to promote.

Whatever the goals of the student, the quality of the instructor must be considered, as well as the proficiency of his students. One important value to promote good study is morale. An exhibition I once saw at Roger Tsung's *wu shu* academy was impressive to me not only for the great skills of his students, but for their happy dispositions. They smiled all the time they were working.

A style should not have self-imposed limitations. It should enhance freedom and not restrict any kind of physical, mental or spiritual development. The long-range movements help one to reach out, to expand beyond one's limitations. Any style a student adopts should embrace this principle, perhaps above all else.

Short and restricted movement inhibits thinking and action. Restricted thought and action narrows one's attitude toward life as a whole, makes one guard what little one possesses, and be afraid to extend oneself. The spiritual enlightenment which we desire will not follow. Such individuals will search in vain for a security which can never be found.

The monks at the Shaolin monastery, prompted by the Taoist/Buddhist doctrine of indivisibility of mind and body, developed and practiced kung fu for the purpose of physical and mental development. The physical training was intended to develop strength, flexibility, relaxation, coordination and agility. It was not necessary to practice striking at each other to develop their high degree of fighting skills. Oneness of mind and body naturally became a forceful means of protection. Self-defense was a by-product of the self-awareness the teachings produced.

The famous Animal styles were developed later, not, it is said, to imitate the fighting techniques of the animals, but to bring the mind and body closer to nature. Nevertheless, there is this story concerning the beginnings of the Praying Mantis style, according to legend, the first Animal style to be developed.

It is said there was once a great warrior whose name was Wong Long. His prowess was unparalleled, and everywhere he was acknowledged to be the Master. He was always looking for a new challenge, to test his superiority. Once, having defeated a formidable opponent, and revelling in his own power, he heard his vanquished foe say, "You think you are a great fighter, Wong Long, because you have defeated me; but to be the true champion, you must defeat the humble monks of the Shaolin monastery, for they are truly the greatest fighters of all."

"Who are these Shaolin?" Wong Long asked. "How may I find them, and defeat them?"

"They are in the North, at the foot of Shangshon Mountain. But it will avail you nothing to find them, for they cannot be defeated." The wounded warrior gasped, and breathed his last.

The arrogant Wong Long travelled far, and everywhere he went he heard of these great fighters. Finally, he came to the steps of the Shaolin monastery. He banged on the gate and demanded entrance. The gate was opened by a humble servant with a broom.

Wong Long made clear his intention to defeat the monastery's greatest champion, whereupon the servant laughed in his face and, with incredible ease, threw the great warrior out onto the road and slammed the gate in his face.

The warrior travelled wide again, and spent years studying to improve his skills until he had become surely the greatest fighter the world had ever seen. He returned to the temple and, being confronted by the same servant, defeated him easily, then proceeded to do the same with all the monks of the temple until, finally, he confronted the Grand Master, who easily bested him. Again he was thrown out onto the road.

In despair, the warrior walked into the desert and sat disconsolately meditating upon his failure. While sitting, he observed before him a praying mantis, battling with a beetle. He became fascinated with the technique of the mantis. He took up a little stick and poked at the beast, so as to observe its technique better. Finally, he developed a dance, in which he emulated the mantis, in all its prowess, speed and cunning.

He returned to the temple and issued his challenge again. All the monks fell away from him in fear until, finally, he confronted the Grand Master. They fought, and his innovative Praying Mantis techniques proved superior. He beat back the Master relentlessly. However, at the last, the Master, having learned from

David Carradine.
Photo © Bob Kuhn.

Wong Long while fighting with him, had managed to assimilate his techniques and was able to defeat him. Wong Long, at this point, gave up his arrogant quest and offered himself into the service of the temple, bringing, thereby, the tai chi Praying Mantis style of Shaolin fighting into being.

The key in this story, and where the power lies, is not in the lowly praying mantis, but in the act of assimilation, requiring openness, and in the state of humility which Wong Long in the end achieved.

The study of the Animal styles, notably the Tiger, Leopard, Snake, Crane, Monkey, Eagle, Mystical Dragon and Praying Mantis, helps us to become open, natural and more efficient in our movements. Animals have a perfect, natural sense of balance, relaxation and agility which civilized humans lack. Primitive people possess much of the same natural rhythm of motion as do wild animals. Children have natural movements, but lose them as they are influenced by adults.

It is not unusual for a seeker to try, and even to become proficient in several styles. For some this works, for others it doesn't. Be careful about this approach. The idea is not to become an encyclopedia. Too much jumping around can be counter-productive. Jack of all styles, master of none.

I have done quite a bit of experimenting in judo, karate and in various related and unrelated arts and sciences. Fast draw, fencing, gymnastics, trampoline, tap dance, ballet, equitation, race and stunt driving, bicycle, basketball, track and field, mountain climbing, swimming, diving, aerobatic flying. Guitar, piano, sitar, dilruba, harmonica, flute, saxophone, drums, conga, sculpture, painting, calligraphy, folk medicine, animal husbandry, reading, writing, woodworking and mechanics.

I have practiced a certain amount of pure street fighting out of necessity, some of which became fairly serious. While in the army, I was exposed to other forms of combat. All of this has stood me in good stead.

As has always been the case with me in all endeavors, I took what I wanted. I did not precisely *learn* the Tiger Crane, or a judo form; but I *know* them, in the sense that I have assimilated them and they are now part of my spacious, ever expanding candy store of useful flavors.

Still, I have always come back to the Northern Shaolin and the teachings of Sifu Kam Yuen. But, I have actually never left. I made a commitment to this road a long time ago. The truth is: my style is my own. I study various formal systems which I can drape on my body and wear like clothes. I use what suits me. I express myself with my own speed and rhythm. Certain techniques, in which I am especially interested, I learn precisely and formally, sometimes again and again, never getting enough. These include the Law Horn, Shaolin, Mantis, ling po, tai chi, and the twelve combination exercises. For the most part, I move ahead freely, spontaneously, learning off the top of my head and through the tips of my toes.

Think not so much of disciplining the mind and body as of releasing them.

6

*They come and
go and draw
from the well.
If one gets
almost down to
the water
And the rope
does not go all
the way,
Or the jug
breaks, it brings
misfortune.*

*One should not
drink the mud
of a well.
No animals
come to an old
well.*
I Ching

CHANGE

We have come here to better ourselves. We can't do this and still remain the same as we were. We must change, starting now and continuing to do so from here on out. When this process of change ceases, progress stops, crystallization sets in, decay inevitably follows.

Change is the one constant in this world of constant change. This is an acknowledged fact in Chinese thought, in quantum mechanics, in cosmic theory and in combat strategy. The second law of thermodynamics states that the amount of activity can not decrease, it can only increase, which basically means that there *is* no standing still. We either progress or we deteriorate.

The redundant attempts not to change. It repeats and repeats. Static. Without self-awareness, the flexible is at a disadvantage. Flexibility becomes planetary to the static; revolving around it, continually changing in an effort to find a way to relate constructively. Eventually, the flexible finds the "proper" stance, and communication of a sort is established. The flexible has become subordinate to the static, revolving around it slavishly. To avoid this situation requires creative self-motivation. You have to break away.

To say, "My style has not changed in three hundred years," and be proud of this fact indicates stagnation. *My* style changed just a moment ago, as a result of writing that sentence, and I hope for it to change again right away.

A style, like anything else, has to constantly improve from generation to generation, or from moment to moment, for that matter; not because "new" is better, but because each moment has left its mark on the next so that we need not repeat the same mistakes and inadequacies, and so that we can change with the changes.

Modern training methods and nutrition make people today potentially more knowledgeable, stronger, faster in mind and body than ever before. We are, so to speak, standing on our ancestors' shoulders. We need teachers who can motivate us to new heights, unlock our spiritual potential—not systems which restrict us to antique levels of performance. Awareness of the past should serve the present and shape the future and not enslave us. The spirit and the essence of the art are what matter, not the prescribed sequence of steps or the names of the categories, forms, positions or techniques.

Newer and better training methods are bound to emerge if we encourage them. The power, glory, the essence and the history of the arts need to be honored and preserved; but the methods and applications need to change for the better, and new ideas need to be encouraged. We need not safeguard the past at all costs, but expand upon it. If we do not change, we can not improve and we will fall backward, as there is no standing still. Tradition has much to teach us. However, it must serve our needs and not become our master. Kung fu is a forever-growing art form. It will always have room for improvement.

It is vital that dedicated individuals and collective groups continue to expand and spread their knowledge for the furtherance of the art, rather than wasting energy and effort contending with the accomplishments of the past or protecting the status quo through the repression of original thought. Training methods and techniques are not carved in stone. There is still something left to be said by us latter-day mortals.

This is not to say that the last word has been spoken in regard to the traditional approaches to martial arts. We are not about to reject the old Masters. What is needed is a reawakening of lost ideals and natural principles, coupled with radical new techniques and procedures. There exists, engraved within the collective unconscious of the human race, forgotten knowledge always ready to surface into the conscious. All we need do is to tap into our own inner selves through techniques which are readily available to us.

Artificial lifestyles and arrogance have caused us to lose touch with the ancient wisdoms. Fear and complacency keep us from breaking free. Knowledge and wisdom do not come from man's distorted intellect but through our ability to discover and accept the natural and simple truth of our place in the cosmos.

Kung fu as a concept and an idea never ceases to evolve. It continues to grow, expand and mature. It can only germinate in a vessel of experience, warmed with the spirit of innovation, encouraged by faithful enthusiasm, dedication and commitment.

7

SELF-DEFENSE

*The enemy is
fear. We think
it is hate; but, it
is fear.*
Gandhi

*Show me a man
of violence that
came to a good
end, and I will
take him for my
teacher.*
Lao tzu

The by-product of self-defense is so interesting to most people that it has eclipsed the central meaning and importance of the art of kung fu. The idea of having some secret knowledge that makes one invincible in battle is the main image people have. This shows how much fear and hate there is in the world.

A true kung fu Master is one who never fights, but always practices.

Everybody on this Earth needs an activity, whether it's playing the guitar, or repairing a car or doing crossword puzzles. These are all ways of examining the fabric of the universe so that we can begin to understand how it works. Most activities require a subject and an object. In the practice of real kung fu the subject and the object are the same thing—oneself. So, then, there is no opponent, or, perhaps more important, there need be none.

Meditate on this and perceive the remarkable change it makes in everything. Without the sense of adversary, where is the problem. Where is the conflict? Why fear? Why hate? Anger? How can there be failure? Why do these things exist at all in a self-contained, sane organism? They certainly are not needed.

What would be the purpose for one who is cosmically aware, who is one with nature, to engage in

Double front kick. David Carradine's signature kick.
Photograph © Michael Lamont.

hand-to-hand combat with his fellow men? These are things to be eliminated in our lives, not encouraged.

Traditional Shaolin kung fu teachings do not encourage fighting or competition. There are no examinations or belts of rank. Students are treated as individuals, moving at their own levels and at their own paces. Prowess and progress are gauged internally.

As far as self-defense goes, the confidence and insight which come from gaining the knowledge of one's own body will turn away all but the most determined efforts at aggression with ease. There is no real need for violent action.

One very important aspect of proficiency in kung fu and in all phases of life is *purposefulness*—the ability to act deliberately rather than arbitrarily. Most of us spend our lives in a random fashion, reacting to stimuli without thinking, as though we were chemicals in a compound, instead of creatures of free will. Kung fu teaches us to choose, to have the power to see all the alternatives and to act according to our own wills rather than on the whims of other people or events. This power is much more useful for self-defense than are mere kicks and punches.

A kung fu Master will usually not waste his time with someone who is interested only in self-defense. When such people appear, Sifu will usually tell them to carry a big stick and not bother him. The Sifu prefers to teach small classes of dedicated disciples and leave the business of instructing poorly motivated students, who are interested only in fighting, to someone else. In kung fu one can be a student, a disciple, a Master or a Grand Master—the disciple is often like the "son" of his Sifu; should the Sifu call in the middle of the night and ask for something, the disciple will do it—this sort of response is not expected of the casual student.

There is no secret technique that will make you invincible. There will always be an individual or circumstance that will best you. This is the nature of things. You seek out this outcome when you concentrate on aggression or defense. It's called looking for trouble. It will find you if you look for it.

Don't, however, become a slave to this attitude. I have just said, you must choose. You have to be yourself. If you want to spar, or kick the big bag, do it. If you have to fight, fight. Get it out of you. You can certainly go a long way with this approach. You must follow your own heart. There is room here for every kind of seeker. Everything furthers. There will always be time later on to pick up on what you've missed.

Lao tzu says, "He who knows how to live can walk abroad without fear of rhinoceros or tiger. He will not be wounded in battle, for in him rhinoceroses can find no place to thrust their horn, tigers no place to use their claws, and weapons no place to pierce. Why is this so? Because he has no place for death to enter." This is the kind of Master to strive to be. The key is *knowing how to live*. This is what we teach.

With the power of kung fu comes a danger which requires spiritual training to overcome, namely, to avoid manipulating people and events to our own advantages. The simplest example of this responsibility is the credo which states that the power must only be used in self-defense. Even this statement falls short of the ideal. The true goal is doing good, improving (yourself and others), teaching, healing.

This is one reason why the kung fu Master does not push the student hard, and says very little. The student must find these convictions in his own heart and in her own time, or they will mean very little, and be misused.

In the past, kung fu teachings were kept secret from all but the initiated. This secrecy was designed to keep the power out of the hands of unscrupulous practitioners. Regrettably, this exclusivity is no longer practiced by most teachers. In many cases the teachers themselves were taught wrongly in the first place. As a result, the art is often used for bad purposes and teachings are passed on to more and more detriment. The art, or parts of it, is taught to police, soldiers, terrorists, drug dealers and criminals in general. This was never meant to be.

When kung fu was taught only by the monks, the teachings could be controlled, and the Masters and students monitored. Now anyone who wants to can hang out a sign that says "kung fu taught here," no matter how little he knows or what his intentions. This results in crudely trained fighters without the perspective of philosophy, and causes the spread of many misconceptions concerning the art.

Can you, concentrating on your breathing, make it soft like that of a child? This is called the mysterious power.

Soft and weak overcome hard and strong. Fish cannot leave deep waters, And a country's weapons should not be displayed. Tao abides in non-action, Yet nothing is left undone.
Lao tzu

CHI

Chi, or internal power, is perhaps *the* most fascinating and mysterious aspect of martial arts training. The nature of chi is difficult to grasp. It is the power that comes from within, not simply for combat, but for all endeavors, and for balance, health, and longevity. Chi can be translated as inner strength or vital force. It is in the mind, in the spirit, and in the body. Chi is sense of power and self-mastery, the drawing of energy from the universe through the subconscious. This inner, vital strength is not dependent on, or even related to, size or physique.

Without some chi strength, life itself is impossible. When chi is abundant, one has true power. Disease and depression vanish. Longevity is increased.

Chi is not readily learned as a solely physical skill. More often, it cultivates itself, as a natural by-product of months and years of training. Although all the training develops chi to some extent, there are specific exercises that develop chi strength. Still, it is better not to know these special techniques until you have learned to control chi power.

That said, the simplest exercise to develop chi passively is stance training. The holding of a stance concentrates the chi. Usually a horse stance or a forward stance is employed, but any stance will do. A toe stance or one-legged stance is very effective as balance becomes a factor. Do not employ the stance rigidly or you will produce the wrong effect. Rock, roll the hips and shoulders, move the arms, within the stance. Feel the power. Taste it.

Extensive stance training, incidentally, has other effects. It develops stability and poise. It can also lead to the creation of strength in the bones and ligaments, the kind of strength that can virtually do away with accidental injury.

Deep breathing exercises, particularly the exercise known as Gigong meditation, and the practice of flowing movements along with mental control drills are the usual means of developing the chi. The continuous movement of the kung fu forms promote the concentration and tranquility necessary for the development of chi power. The mind, or rather, the will directs, and the body acts. The resultant energy and power is concentrated in a single direction. The final force is much more powerful than simple muscle strength alone. It is an energy-controlling thought and a thought-controlling energy. Under certain conditions, the mind can control this energy flow in the body *and* in the immediate outside environment, as well.

The blow that does not touch and Bruce Lee's famous two-inch punch are two lowly examples of this phenomenon.

This energy is the basis of acupuncture science. There appears to be another circulatory system within the body, a network of energy fields. Blockage of the energy flow results in pain, weakness and sickness. The acupuncture needle releases the blockage and congestion, restoring the energy flow.

The chi can only exist in the absence of fear or tension. These factors create imbalance. When relaxed, one is not in upheaval. One can concentrate and see clearly what it is that needs to be done, and do it naturally, spontaneously, and instantaneously.

The chi will not flow freely through a stressed, weak or sick body. Wherever the body is tight or constricted, the flow of the chi will stop.

The internal Shaolin styles of tai chi chuan, pa kua and hsing i are based more or less entirely on the use of chi. The study of these styles is the most direct way of passively developing the chi, as is to a smaller extent the practice of any slow-motion exercise. The point is to focus one's concentration into oneself and create a positive loop of energy which feeds upon itself. Performing the tai chi form will produce this effect every time.

As the chi develops within, control is vitally important. A casual tap with the fingers can do serious injury once the chi is strong. One must be very careful. Emotional content, such as anger, or fear, or even just excitement, can bring the chi unbidden to the hand.

For this reason, the seeker waits until proficiency in meditation, tranquility and the art of non-reaction have been established before one goes on to more specific, advanced chi training.

These rules are to keep the seeker out of trouble. Respect them and you can't go wrong.

Recently, in Beijing, China, researchers have been applying the scientific method to chi, in an effort to discover the nature of the phenomenon. This has resulted in documentation of the amazing feats accomplished by Gigong Masters, as they are called, which include, among other things, imperviousness to blows with stones and swords, and the curing of acute and chronic illnesses.

These studies have determined that the chi is not psychic in nature, as was previously believed, but actual, empirical energy that flows through the body on pathways of extremely high electrical conductivity. Gigong breathing and meditation increase the conductivity by producing acetylcholine.

Acupuncture stimulates the channels by tapping directly into them. When the pathways are clear and in good condition the chi flows smoothly, and health and strength follow.

MEDITATION

One day Kam said, "Why don't you meditate? That's what it's all about David." So I sat down and tried. I was more or less missing for about an hour. I flew. I came back to Earth a different man. This seemed like something I should get into further. I didn't really have the time for a full commitment to regular meditation. Consequently, I evolved a technique of meditating for an instant at a time, anywhere and anytime I wanted. I started doing it twenty or thirty times a day. As I said, I was a natural.

Meditation is more than important. For some it is the sole objective and the primary goal, the total purpose of study. Proponents of meditation generally believe that events and probabilities can be determined and altered for the better by the exercise of this power.

The best possible time to meditate is right after exercising. Kung fu dancing stimulates the adrenal glands and the para-nervous systems, heightening awareness and raising the level of excitement. In this state we are especially open to the power of meditation. Dancing also uses up acetylcholine, which is the electrical conductor between the individual synapses of the nervous system. Meditation rebuilds acetylcholine and quiets the adrenals and para-nervous system. Dancing and sitting. A real yin-yang situation.

Caine, at his most inscrutable.
© 1972 Warner Bros. Inc.
All Rights Reserved

The nervous system is what we think with, not just the brain, but the whole nervous system. It is all connected, down to the tips of the fingers and toes. The stomach probably does more thinking than does the brain. Hunger can easily override the highest ideals. Concentration on controlling these factors leads to the center of awareness and increases the power of the meditation exercise.

Sit down on the floor or the ground right where you are and close the eyes. Make the breathing regular and quiet the heart. Empty the mind. Concentrate on The One Thing, then forget it. You are meditating.

The active and passive meditations of kung fu practice bring peace, calmness, a feeling of release, liberation, detachment from common, everyday burdens, mind and body working as one. Ecstasy. Through this experience one becomes a better person and, of oneself, chooses not to abuse the power one has developed. Relaxed rhythmic movement and stillness are the direct cause of this ecstasy. Creative, constructive thought follows, directed by the mind and the will, not by the emotions and the stomach. Once this state begins to occur frequently, you can expect it to recur at will.

Remember always that this is a technique, not a goal. Do not lose sight of the infinite nature of your search. Meditation is not an answer; it is only a useful question and a poor, humble pastime. The path leads to the Way. *That* is what we're trying to get to. Once the Way is found, there is no longer a need for the path. Nirvana is, after all, a dead end.

There is no destination. Not on this Earth. There is only the journey. If you forget that these things are *tools,* you will be caught, and forget the quest.

Some have managed to do this;
they have hit the true center, and then?
Very few have been able to stay there.

The process is not understood.
The men of talent shoot past it,
and the others do not get to it.
Confucius

THE KNOWLEDGE

Philosophy means, literally, "love of knowledge," but learning knowledge for the sake of knowledge is simply another kind of pleasure seeking. Knowledge needs a goal besides itself. "Kung fu philosophy" translates as "love of knowledge of knowing what to do."

The foundation of all knowledge is study. To start out right, and to continue to proceed in the right direction, the seeker of knowledge must read. Movies and television have their place, but reading deals with words as symbols, which is the way our brain deals with words.

At the end of this book, there is a short reading list to help the seeker. It is a brief list. There is much more out there, but you will have to find it for yourself. Meanwhile, some special writings are mentioned here. They are an integral part of my own learning, and I pass them on to you.

These are not how-to books on martial arts, but deep and, for the most part, profound works on the essential nature of the universe. Some of them are difficult, and some are virtually recreational. Some are works of fiction and fantasy. There's no law that says serious study can't be fun. I got some of my basic philosophical understanding from comic books.

The Chinese written language, with its more than five hundred characters, is not made up of symbols for sounds but of images. Each character has no one simple meaning but is instead many concepts, pictures and ideas. For this reason, no written Chinese sentence can be exactly defined or translated. There will always be more than one meaning.

Tradition has added curlicues of ornamentation to the Chinese language characters which make them seem obscure. Ancient Chinese writing is simpler and much easier to feel.

Most of us here will have to make do with English, but we can consider ourselves lucky, since English has the largest and most flexible vocabulary of them all.

Even so, reading won't carry us the whole distance. These mysteries are so deep, there are sometimes no words to describe them. A kung fu teacher will not speak of them. He will talk, if he speaks at all, of other things, little things like techniques, tricks and immediate goals.

The student has to find the important ideas in the silence of his or her own mind, as he or she practices and meditates.

Here are the books:

Study of the *I Ching* is essential. The *I Ching* is composed of 64 symbols called hexagrams. Hexagrams are figures of six lines—some of which are solid, unbroken lines (yang lines) and some of which are broken (yin lines). The lines and the hexagrams they form represent the cosmos and forces of change. The Shaolin techniques are all related to the seasons, the elements, forces of change and universal phenomena. All these things are defined in the *I Ching* and explained in the commentaries that accompany the hexagrams.

Apparently, there were four authors of the *I Ching*. Fu Hsi and King Wen are, alternately, credited with inventing the hexagrams that are at the core of the book. The earliest written versions of the book are approximately 4,000 years old. The present version was set down by King Wen and his son, the Duke of

Chou around 1200 B.C. Confucius appears to have contributed his commentaries to the text in 600 B.C.

People often use the *I Ching* as a fortune-telling device. While this is an amusing, and perhaps informative, way to study the book, it does not begin to unlock the depth and the breadth of knowledge the *I Ching* contains if it is studied for its own sake.

Tao Te Ching by Lao tzu, and *The Inner Chapters* by Chuang-tzu are at the bedrock of Taoist philosophy. These works are the place to go for a basic feel and understanding of Chinese thought.

Wei Wu Wei is a pen name that was used by many monks over the centuries when they wanted to write about the mysteries of non-volitional living of *action* in *non-action*. Their *All Else Is Bondage* is presently out of print in English, but it still can be found. A very advanced book, this work examines, and attempts to define, a non-objective universe, free of industry and desire, where all is *One*. It is a very small book but takes years to understand.

The Tibetan Book of the Dead gives a complete, though terrifying, picture of the bridge between life and death. It offers, incidentally, a good description of the madness that is the human mind. This may seem irrelevant, but it is anything but that. From understanding of these things comes much of the ability to discover, control and direct the hidden powers within us.

Fritjof Capra's *The Tao of Physics* is a Western book which explains Taoist teaching in terms of quantum theory mechanics, and vice versa, making both more accessible.

Ying Zi and Weng Yi's *Shaolin Kung Fu* is presently out of print. This coffee table book contains a great deal of information about the growth of the art. It includes a good historical background and many photographs and paintings.

Sun and Steel, by Yukio Mishima, is the inspirational first-hand account of one extraordinary man's transformation from a bookish intellectual into a dazzlingly powerful warrior-philosopher. Bronzing and sculpting his body with sun-bathing, weight lifting and martial arts, Mishima became a samurai prophet with thousands of disciples.

He later became a dissident activist and ended his life in martyrdom, after an aborted coup in which he attempted to rally the army behind his revolution, devoted to the return of the Japanese culture from materialistic obsession to the traditional ideals of honor, war and poetry. He performed public *hara-kiri* with his number one disciple and lover acting as his second and dying with him. A pure and exotic marvel of Zen extremism.

Heraclitus's work is full of provocative observations on the way things really are, generally refuting the mundane attitudes of strict logicians. Only about one hundred fragments of his thought—put down around 500 B.C.—still exist. Nonetheless, students are supposedly still capable of spending years haggling over his theories. Though his work is integral to the study of Western philosophy, his paradoxical logic and his notions regarding *the One* make his teaching similar, in certain ways, to Taoism.

BOOK THREE

THE LESSONS

1

WHY
KUNG FU?

There is a great desire in all people for self-improvement on every level: physical, mental and spiritual, as well as economic and social. Every one of us would improve the quality of our existence if we could. Well, we can. Countless avenues are available to us. The question is which to choose. Physical programs abound. Self-help books and spiritual tracts are all over the place. We have to know what works, and on what level. What are our real goals in these pursuits? How far will they take us? Will they hurt us? Will they hold our interest? Will they provide us with the tools enabling us to focus our wills on the task?

I'm going to assume anyone who reads this is interested in something deep and more or less all-encompassing.

Aerobics, weight lifting and jogging all have something going for them. On the other hand, bouncing around to loud music, the strain and pain of pumping iron, shin splints and low back pain from pounding on pavement, and tension and tedium are not exactly what we're looking for. And where is the development of mind and spirit in these pursuits? Not there in any big way.

All these activities are just that: activities. Two weeks at any of them and there's not much more to

In dealing with persons as intractable and as difficult to influence as a pig or a fish, the whole secret of success depends on finding the right approach.
I Ching

By their stillness, they become sages;
By their movements, Kings.
Lao tzu

learn. From there it's a question of repetition and gradual improvement (or deterioration).

There is another aspect which I believe is the whole point—overall improvement of the texture and quality of life.

Kung fu study can give you this. I'm talking about serenity, lack of tension, heightened awareness, greater moral fiber, increased willpower, less fatigue, better understanding of oneself and one's environment, better social relations, confidence, material success, oneness with nature, freedom from fear, anxiety and boredom, resistance to illness, freedom from vice, increased longevity and the ability to kick ass.

And it's easy to do. Fun, actually. Uplifting, and more or less eternally rewarding. You can pursue kung fu studies for twenty years or a lifetime and you will never stop learning something new every day. The teachings will infect your daily life in every way.

If you are really dedicated about it, and dedication is one of the gifts it gives you, it will lead you to all kinds of unlooked-for accomplishments. You will sharpen your awareness and your perception. You will become conversant with art, music, literature, general knowledge. You will become both a realist and a mystic. You will hold the world around you together with your strength and wisdom.

Sounds like an impossible panacea, doesn't it? But don't get me wrong, it's not a free ride. You get only what you earn. On the other hand, any little bit you absorb is going to improve things.

You don't have to give up the way you live for this. In fact, it's better if you don't. The magic needs to work on you as you are. Keep pumping iron or jogging if you really want to. Show up once a week or once a month. Don't practice. There's no rule against the casual kung fu artist. Who knows, maybe the call will come to you later on. Or, maybe you'll walk away at some point, taking with you all that you've learned and become.

If you want to go all the way and have the will to do it, there's that too. It can be pretty exciting. It may not be for you.

The ideas contained in these teachings are simple and powerful, suggestive, quick and easy, yet larger than life and, paradoxically, difficult to comprehend.

This is the way and the nature and the practice of gung fu—the essence and the power. It is here for you if you choose to reach out and take it.

2

Green plants are tender and filled with sap. At their death they are withered and dry. A tree that is unbending is easily broken.

The Tao of Heaven is to take from those who have too much, And give to those who do not have enough.
Lao tzu

KUNG FU AS HEALING

 Since kung fu is not merely a fighting, religious or philosophical discipline but a *way of life,* naturally, among its accomplishment techniques is a system of healing.

The study of kung fu alone will promote good health, and strong minds and bodies, but more dynamic methods are available, as well. The use of special massages and pressures, herbs and tinctures, corrective and healing movements and stances, and certain mystical disciplines, having to do with meditation and divination, all of which can be tailored to benefit specific viscera, organs, maladies and conditions, are part of any Master's general knowledge. I've already spoken of Sifu Kam Yuen's Master, Tsu Chu Kai, who was able to heal and reshape shattered bones through massage, working the bits and splinters together and using gentle pressure to knit the fibers to each other.

Li Ching Yuen, a legendary kung fu nutritionist who is reputed to have lived for 256 years, was responsible for the discovery of many such cures, the most famous of which is an herbal mixture called "Fo Ti Tieng," said to have great regenerative powers, and thought to be at least partly responsible for his longevity. There are products available in health food stores with that name; however, the true formula is kept secret.

Everybody knows about ginseng. Ginseng is a root which grows wild. It takes seven years for the plant to fully develop its root, which when fully mature has a human form. Cultivated varieties are not of much value, since the plant needs some hardship to develop its healing powers. Red ginseng is an energizer, while cooked white ginseng has a tranquilizing effect. The plant has many beneficial side effects, mostly related to balancing the enzymes and secretions; these attributes are common to both kinds. The best variety, according to the Koreans, Russians and Chinese, is wild American ginseng, found mainly in the deep South—although the Americans insist on the Korean, Siberian and Chinese varieties.

Many of the Chinese curative techniques have been ignored or ridiculed in the West for centuries. Only recently have Western doctors begun to give some partial credibility to these methods. For example, acupuncture is now accepted as a pain killer, though the more important healing aspects are still regarded doubtfully. Chinese philosophy and knowledge in general have suffered from the same skepticism. This prejudice dates back to the ancient Greeks who, in their zeal to neatly categorize the cosmos, attempted to eliminate anything which could not be explained empirically.

One example of the kind of prescription which is bound to be rejected by Westerners is an herbal tincture called *tieh teh jieuw,* pronounced "dih dah jaow." This preparation is widely used by Chinese martial artists to alleviate and prevent the sore muscles, ligaments, tendons and bones that result from hard training. It also has some effect against arthritis, and has been known to correct conditions over which conventional medicine was powerless. Taken internally, it works on some organs and acts as a tonic. A few ounces taken before a match will provide extra energy and prevent bruising.

The formula consists of twenty-seven separate ingredients—animal, vegetable and mineral—the preparation of which is a discipline in itself. It's easy to see why a medical doctor would have a hard time believing in a cure which contained, as part of its ingredients, powdered eagle's claw and a live snake. These sorts of cures are generally regarded by the scientific community on about the same level as astrology or palmistry.

It's not the purpose of this book to educate the reader in esoteric cures. However, the student will come across these things as he progresses, perhaps to his advantage. More to the point, and less explicable, is the healing effect of the studies themselves. Go to class. Get well.

3

NUTRITION

No, Son; you can't have a cigarette until you finish your vegetables.
Gail McCool

Good mental and physical health, strength and longevity, even good emotional shape, are dependent on proper nutrition. It is impossible to speak about this area at all without getting involved with all the various fads which surround the subject.

Good, healthy, balanced meals are the basic ingredient, but there is vast disagreement on just what that is. Let us begin with eliminating the obviously bad. It's become a standard view that meat and potatoes aren't enough. Conventionally fried foods are out. Junk foods are junk. This gives us a good start. The best nutrition is to be obtained from fresh, if possible raw, fruits and vegetables. Meat, fish and fowl should be approached carefully. Dairy is spoken out against by many experts. I personally do not ascribe to that theory. Eggs are very controversial. Salt and sugar used in abundance are poisons.

Recent studies in China, where a huge population with vastly different eating habits can be compared, have shown that a predominantly vegetarian diet will definitely lower cholesterol levels, decrease the incidence of heart disease, cancer, gastric problems, organ failures and increase longevity. It seems that the human species is really constructed to eat berries, nuts, leaves, roots, grubs, insects and an occasional fish.

Another factor to be considered, however, is the matter of what our ancestors have eaten. Successive generations of a certain kind of eating produce an evolutionary tendency which cannot be denied. A descendant of Viking warriors (who were used to big chunks of rare meat) might not fare well on brown rice and seaweed.

Vitamins and mineral supplements can be a big help and a big pitfall. Not only can vitamins be overdone to bad effect, but improper formulation or preparation can cause them to actually weaken the subject. There seems to be no reliable information about which ones are good and which ones aren't. Kinesiology purports to be able to analyze the effectiveness of vitamins and supplements, if you can accept that.

The best source of vitamin and mineral intake is undoubtedly healthy natural foods and an extensive program of herbs.

If you want to get fancy, there are all the amino acids, and such things as raw organ extracts, which work on the theory that if your pancreas needs help, eat pancreas. It's worth trying, if your budget can handle it.

There are some specific tricks you can play with your diet if you're careful not to go overboard. Vince Gironda, of Vince's Gym, who has been my body building guru for twenty-five years or so, recommends a vegetarian reducing diet for weight loss, which consists mainly of salads. By salads I mean raw green and yellow vegetables with unsaturated oils and lemon juice for dressing. This regimen will strip it off you. To develop a lean and mean muscular body, he prescribes raw meat and water. This is a dangerous diet. It is lacking in all the vitamins and minerals, and you're likely to start acting like a hungry tiger around the house. Six weeks of this regimen, supplemented with vitamins and minerals, is the maximum he recommends. Then, carry on a normal diet for a while before hitting it again. Watch your temper!

My brothers and I have a recipe for a body-builder's snack. It consists of raw chunks of beef, marinated with olive oil, garlic, lemon juice, and chopped onions. We eat it with our fingers, and then go out and kick the bag. We call it "Tarzan food." It always disappears very quickly.

Vegetarianism is a long-accepted diet for spiritual clarity, physical health and potential longevity. This does not mean eating a lot of eggplant casserole and macaroni. It means raw, or simply cooked fruits and vegetables, whole grains, nuts and seeds.

There are many different diets which are called "vegetarian," such as those including fish or chicken. Lacto-vegetarianism includes dairy products. Vegan means no animal products, whatsoever. Fruitarian means, obviously, nothing but fruit. I've experimented with them all. "Nothing that runs away when you try to eat it" is a good one. "Nothing with two eyes and a mouth." That one lets in clams and oysters. In these diets, ideas about good nutrition are getting mixed up with moral or ethical considerations, or flights of fancy. One can get lost here. Or one can get found.

Food combining is another thing you can pay attention to. It is based on the thought that the less trouble you give your body in the way of food processing, the freer it will be to concentrate on other things, like regeneration and healing. Some foods digest in different parts of your alimentary canal. There's nothing to be gained by confusing your body by dumping a lot of different things into your stomach. For instance, concentrated proteins and carbohydrates and starches don't go well together, because they require different enzymes from you for digestion.

There's a thing called the "mucusless" diet that makes a lot of sense to me. It says you should keep all the stuff that tends to gum up your body out of your body. Arnold Ehrat, who wrote the book on the diet, unfortunately didn't get the chance to personally prove its long-term value. He was run over by an Armour meat truck in the prime of his life.

Finally, there is fasting. It definitely has its uses.

Without outside nourishment, our body uses what it can find. It starts out with the stored fats and other junk lying around, disposing of stored toxins as well. (This can be a problem, at first, because the toxins are initially released into your system, where they can do harm.) Extreme fasting will have you losing muscle mass as well as fat, since when you run out of your emergency stores, you begin cannibalizing muscle. A way around this is to fast with a liquid amino acid supplement. You'll slim down and still retain your strength. Eventually, fasting will start to cannibalize your non-vital organs and also cause you to develop anemia. So, while fasting can do some good, can even save your life, it can also kill you if it turns from fasting into starvation.

The best rule is moderation, a certain amount of abstinence and an ascetic approach to food. Stop eating for entertainment. I know the healthiest I ever felt was when I was on a diet of fresh juice, fruits and vegetables. I ate gigantic salads and was lean and strong. I had lots of energy and needed very little sleep. The only problem I had was that I couldn't stick to it.

4

STRETCHING

*Float like the clouds:
Drift with the wind.*
Master Po

The first thing to achieve, before techniques, or power, or any of the rest of it, is flexibility. When a beginner looks to develop strength, one always thinks in terms of muscle flex. This is only half of it. The stretch of a muscle is just as important. Ignoring this aspect results in muscle-boundness. Most students stretch simply to loosen up, so as not to strain the muscles during a workout. This, again, is only half of it. To achieve maximum flexibility, stretching must become a deep process.

Once I said to Sifu, "I can't touch my toes without bending my knees." He said, "Bend your knees." I tried this. With my knees bent, I grasped my feet and forced my legs to straighten. After a while I achieved a full stretch. Later on, Sifu said, "Why don't you do that sitting down? It's more comfortable." Later on, I found myself sitting, my legs straight, and my whole

Rob Moses demonstrating amazing flexibility in a full stretch.

upper body forward with my chin on the floor between my knees, breathing easily, totally comfortable. I said to Sifu. "I feel as though I'd like to just stretch like this forever." Sifu said, "Now, you're getting it."

Every part of the training, to be fully effective, must be thoroughly pursued as an end in itself.

Don't be in a hurry. Haste will get you there slower, not faster.

5

STANCE TRAINING

Don't just act; stand there.
Elia Kazan

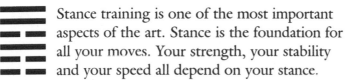 Stance training is one of the most important aspects of the art. Stance is the foundation for all your moves. Your strength, your stability and your speed all depend on your stance.

In the Shaolin temples, traditionally, a student would have to undergo a half-year or so of pure stance training before he would be permitted to begin to learn the moves. These days a new student begins to learn the moves immediately. I was taught very advanced techniques from the very beginning, sometimes only minutes before I would be required to perform them on film.

This kind of study tends to minimize or submerge the importance of stance training. No modern student will ever experience the slow and steady growth that was the norm for the old-style kung fu acolyte. This is a great loss—one we must try to make up for, if we can.

The slow learning of the basic stances provides the foundation from which all the techniques and disciplines of kung fu practice derive.

The Horse Stance: In the old days, a student would practice this and nothing else for six months. Feet apart, somewhat wider than the shoulders, toes slightly spread, legs bent, back straight, shoulders down, arms at sides slightly bent, fists clenched at the waist, eyes straight ahead. Curl the pelvis forward so

Forward Stance.

Reverse Forward Stance.

that the buttocks don't stick out. Accomplish all this and you will have achieved a state of balance. To check the stance, look down and be sure the feet are hidden by the knees. With practice, the stance will become comfortable and easy. Repetition will strengthen you.

Forward Stance: Turn the body to the right, bending the forward knee and straightening the rear leg, turning the front foot to about a forty-five degree angle and the rear a little less. Center the body over the two legs, still keeping the back straight, shoulders down and head up. Again you can check by seeing that your feet are hidden by your knees.

Reverse Forward Stance: Same as above, but facing the other way. Try to accomplish the exchange without disturbing the balance, passing through the horse stance position on the way. Keep it flowing.

Heel Stance: From the forward stance, straighten the front leg, causing all the weight to be transferred to the back leg. Lift the toe of the leading foot, keeping the heel on the ground.

Toe Stance, or Cat Stance: In this stance, all the weight is on the back leg, with that leg slightly bent, the front leg is extended forward, also slightly bent, the toe touching the floor in front. This is potentially the most mobile of all the stances, ready to move or jump in any direction.

Lift the front leg, pointing the toe down, and keeping the raised foreleg perpendicular and close to the body, with the arms held out at the side for balance and you will have accomplished a basic **crane stance**.

There are other stances, but these are the primary ones, and it is the practice of these that will give the student strength, balance and stability, from which to proceed toward the rest of it. Practicing of the stances is supposed to lead to a meditational set of mind, and is absolutely necessary in order to establish the basis from which to develop the techniques that are to follow. You can't kick if you can't stand.

Heel Stance.

Toe Stance.

Crane Stance.

Horse Stance.

Static stance training, in which the student holds the stance still, is only part of it. This exercise, common in most teaching, is a stagnant practice, useful mainly for developing endurance. It makes the student tense and less able to move quickly. Stance should be transitional, flowing from one to another with ease and grace. A stolid stance is a vulnerable stance.

The dynamic method is to strike a stance momentarily, and change smoothly to the next, altering the position of the arms as well. Move slowly from one pose to another without stopping—horse stance, forward stance, toe stance, heel stance—always changing, never static. Drift with the wind, float like the clouds.

None of this dissertation is of much use without an instructor to show you how—touching you here and there to correct and adjust you, illustrating the right and wrong of what you are trying to do. It cannot be learned from a book.

All I'm trying to do here is excite you enough to lead you to a *class*.

THE
CLASS

*Remember you
have come here
having
already
understood the
necessity of
struggling with
yourself.
Therefore thank
everyone who
gives you the
opportunity.*
Gurdjieff

*Siddown and
Shuddup!*
Humphrey
Bogart

 Eventually the student must join a class. There is no way to proceed very far along this path without help. Kung fu cannot be approached alone by an individual. The give and take and community interaction is an absolutely essential requirement.

The choosing of a class should be done carefully. At the beginning, any influence is likely to have a lasting effect. The last thing you want to do is just walk into a place that has a sign out proclaiming "Kung fu Taught Here." Anyone who wants to can put up a sign like that.

The pages of this book cannot choose a Master for you. You have to find him yourself. Listen skeptically to any tales of power, promises of extravagant achievements, or guarantees of success. A good system will always keep it simple, straightforward, plain and prosaic.

Above all, stay away from any place that advertises "Kung fu-karate." There's absolutely no such thing.

Then there is the question of style: what is best for *you*. Personalities enter into it too.

Research. Shop around. Ask, remembering that everyone thinks their Sifu or style is the best. Once involved in a class, students tend to become blind to all others, as well as to the shortcomings of their own teachers. Don't let this happen to you. Stay skeptical and open. Listen to yourself.

Most kwoons teach a beginning, intermediate and advanced class in one session. The class begins with stretching. Stretching is as important as any other single thing. It develops limberness, flexibility, endurance, strength. It protects the body from injuries during class. Stretching is also a period of peaceful meditation. The stretches are numerous, and similar to those performed by other types of athletes, plus many yoga positions and movements, as well as some that are identical to ballet stretches.

During this period of the class you will also practice your breathing. You need to concentrate on breathing as often as you can. Soon, correct breathing will become second nature and overlap into your daily life.

It is a good idea to make a habit of coming to the class early and performing your own warm-ups and stretches unsupervised. This can become a very rich personal moment. This practice will also move Sifu to give special notice to you. It will look a lot like special dedication to him. If this sounds insincere to you, don't worry about it. Go through the motions. The sincerity will come to you.

After the stretching, the class continues with stance training and the practice of basic techniques—kicks, punches and footwork—followed by combinations of these elements. This part of the class is quite rigorous.

Then come the combination exercises—interlocking groups of techniques which forerun the learning of the longer forms. According to Northern Shaolin tradition, twelve of these are taught, though for most students only four are shown. When a seeker shows unusual devotion, another four are revealed. Rarely are the last four presented at all, except to a serious disciple. During this part of the class, the beginning student will stay with the others as far as he has progressed, and then leave off, and watch hungrily

David Carradine and Kam Yuen in Cannes, France.
Photo © Yves Coatsaliou.

while his more advanced colleagues perform the moves he does not yet know.

The next stage of the class is broken up into several categories. The instructor gives individual help to each student at his or her own level. The newcomer continues to learn the exercises, while the intermediate and advanced students work on learning and perfecting forms, advanced techniques and sparring.

Forms are the means toward learning and understanding the different styles of kung fu. There are hundreds of them, plus scores of weapons forms. After the first one or two basic ones, they are learned in no particular order, the pupil and teacher together deciding in which direction the student wishes or needs to proceed.

The foregoing is not a description of every class there is. There are as many methods as there are teachers and students. However, this is pretty much the traditional way to do it.

Some teachers skip the forms entirely, believing this kind of teaching is too structured for maximum individual progress. The main point of the forms is that they present the various styles in a solid, unaltered chunk dating back hundreds, perhaps thousands, of years without change. Since the styles cannot be written down accurately, the forms are the only way we can be sure they are being passed down faithfully.

Outside the class other instruction is given to those who wish and merit it. These advanced wrinkles are taught confidentially for the most part. Here the seeker can really bust loose. Abandoning order and structure at will, reaching to the limit. Flying.

Some of the most happy times I have ever spent were those months and years when Sifu Kam Yuen and I travelled around the world, working out together. I remember particularly one year, I think it was 1977, when we were together in France for the Cannes Film Festival. We lived in a great old hotel on a cliff overlooking the Mediterranean at a place called Cap d'Antibe. There was a garden there of about four acres. During the festival it was filled with famous people and important film and government functionaries.

Each day, Sifu and I would spend many hours working together in a corner of the park, sweating and discussing philosophy. Then we would put on our finery and attend the functions and interviews. We also gave several exhibitions. It was a truly beautiful time, embodying the perfect relationship between disciple and Master.

When this kind of moment comes to you, savor it. Absorb as much as you can. It will not last forever.

WHEN YOU LOSE THE WAY

At some point or another, many students experience a block in their studies. They get stuck on a plateau, apparently unable to progress further. Sometimes this is the fault of the teacher. If this is so, it is time to move on. More often, though, the problem is an internal one, caused by poor learning habits, problems with attitude or personal outside distractions.

Most of us are bullheaded at first. We will learn our forms and techniques our own way, interpreting and adapting the moves to fit our own prejudices and shortcomings. This approach will inevitably fail. We will be confronted with a barrier of our own making, and probably discontinue our study.

If we have the call, we will eventually return, having forgotten most of our techniques, and begin again with more humility and dedication. We must learn all over, almost from the beginning. This is the learning that truly counts. We will see things we never saw before. Our bodies will surprise us with knowledge. Each lesson will come home like a revelation, and we will not forget again.

Fear is the factor that gets in the way at first more than anything—thinking something can't be done and being afraid to try. This fear can last and, given room, can grow. Eventually, it's likely to overcome everything else and stop you cold.

You need faith in yourself and outside encouragement, and something else: courage. This can be developed if you don't have it. It's not easy, though. Can't be found in this or any other book that I know about.

The next obstacle, once fear is conquered, assuming it is, is the opposite: overconfidence—thinking you've got it down, ego, arrogance, the illusion of clarity. This self-delusion could come on you even if you still have the fear, as a coverup. This student usually talks a lot when he should be listening. After all, there's a reason why we were given two ears and only one mouth.

This obstacle is very hard to overcome without some kind of revelation to pull you out of it, usually brought on by a big ego loss—humiliation, derision, extreme indignity, something like that. Not a pleasant prospect, but worth it in the end.

This scenario is like trying to help a hopeless drunk to see the light. Until he does, he'll deny everything, insisting it's the rest of us that are out of it. He's perfect, magnificent even. He's liable to have to hit bottom really hard before he'll turn around, and then, he might be insufferable in the other direction. Some people never seem to learn. What this guy needs is some humility. Among martial artists, he might find someone who can teach him some, the hard way. Better to get it right the first time.

One thing that will get in your way is simply being wrong. Getting the information or the priorities or the values backwards, or upside down or twisted. This can happen a number of ways. Falling in with the wrong company (this can include the teacher), leaving out some important step—such as listening, or practicing or showing up—obstinacy, ignoring or disobeying the teacher when he tells you what you need to do. The only way out of this syndrome, really, is to change your ways, or get out and end your misery.

Any kind of habitual distractions can destroy your progress. Women, drugs, personal problems, self-pity, dissipation of any kind, to name a few—or just plain laziness. For most failures, it's going to be a combination of some or all of these things, or one after another. Self-indulgence does not become a martial artist. There's no way to progress or excel and at the same time cling to vice and weakness.

Don't be completely discouraged. This is just the sort of thing these studies are supposed to help you out with. You're going to have to have some faith in the program, and in yourself. But, hurry up about it. You don't have all the time in the world to do this thing.

The final obstacle that's going to present itself to you will be old age. You'll be too decrepit to pull it off.

GETTING
IT BACK

The *Tibetan Book of the Dead* speaks of the "clear white light" available to all, but rejected by most at the very beginning of the quest. If this is accepted, nothing more needs to be done. For the rest of us, we miss this chance and strive all our lives to achieve the pale secondary yellow light, which illuminates less brightly the same truths. This is the human condition, the tragicomedy of life on Earth.

Ordinarily, there are three ways we learn: through education or example, through meditation or divination or through experience—the most bitter and hardest, and the slowest way, but the best that most of us can do.

To get past all the obstacles and approach the greater goals, one needs all three, at least. But there's a fourth way. Well, there'd have to be, wouldn't there? You could work on all three together, but that's not what I mean; so, call this the fifth way.

Start over.

Break free. People, like everything else, become set in their ways. The human organism exists in a precarious state of balance, crystallized into a static system that resists change, for better or worse.

You can't alter a part of yourself without altering the whole system. If you try to banish one of your unpleasant traits, something equally odious will very likely appear in its place.

There is the example of the absent-minded professor who always forgot his umbrella or his lecture notes. He worked on this flaw and finally cured himself. He no longer forgot things, but he became ill-tempered and irritable. His students and family liked him better before. So he got rid of his ill temper and became an insomniac. Bad traded for bad, like when you bang down one edge of a paint can lid with a hammer and the other side pops up. No gain.

To successfully change any part of yourself, the crystallization has to be done away with. The whole system has to become fluid. Then it can be altered at will.

This fluidity is best achieved through great anguish or ecstasy. A broken heart or a new romance will put you in this condition nicely. Either one will turn you to jelly. A grueling or transcendent series of kung fu sessions can take you toward either state, or both. Meditation can find it for you. Try to remember how you got there in case you backslide later on.

Once you've established this fluid state, disposed of your rigidity and preconceptions, you are capable of doing something about the problems. Conquer fear by facing it. Examine your self-delusions relentlessly for the truth about yourself. Test your conceptions to the limit, and do away with them when they prove false or inadequate. Get rid of the distractions by getting rid of the belief in them.

Surprise yourself. You have no idea of what you are capable until you ask yourself, "Of what am I capable?"

You are at your very best When things are worst.
Starman

Wake up. Or, at least, if you are dreaming, make it *your* dream. If you are living in someone else's dream, and most of us are, then *you* are not the hero.

When you wake up in the morning, you are waking *into* a dream. Stop that!

Abandon your illusions.

Get real.

If none of this works for you, if you've tried as much of it as you can stomach and you're still lost, or if it all sounds like gobbledygook to you, there's one more way to go, which I will mention to make the list complete, though I do so reluctantly:

For the really hard cases, there's a path that sometimes works—*viatsanyu,* or "Straightening by Fire," a desperate, harsh, cruel technique similar to throwing a person off a cliff, and shouting at him to fly or else! In this case, after much pain, to the body and psyche both, it is oneself that does the throwing and shouting. Good luck!

Viatsanyu requires great strength and courage, and is in many ways dangerous, potentially even fatal. Fear is the energy that makes it work—the more the better. There's no telling what kind of a monster this method will create.

It takes a remarkable person to dare attempt the ordeal of *viatsanyu,* much less survive it.

I'm not going to say any more about it. Ask somebody else. It's not my way. If you're the type to try to make a deal with the devil, that choice is probably along this path somewhere. I should know. Forget it is my advice. Go back to your original purpose, back to your lessons. Start over yet again. Pull your various selves together. Refer to your higher power. Collect your resources. Take stock. Examine your methods, get your goals straight, abandon excuses. Focus. Put to work all you have learned to help you through. Above all, don't give up.

You must find your own Way; and you can.

If, in spite of everything, you fail there is one more possibility: reincarnate.

In the Bible it says Man has three score and ten. This is not a limit. It simply means that if you have lived as long as seventy years and still don't get it, you are not required to go on stumbling along in your

What does not destroy me makes me strong.
Nietzsche

worn-out body with your worn-out mind. You are allowed to quit and try again from scratch in another life. They say that some people never learn, but Never is a long time; longer than Forever, which is only Now.

BECOME WHO YOU WANT TO BE

He who conforms to the TAO, and follows the course of the natural process of Heaven and Earth, is able to handle the whole world.
J. Needham quoted in *The Tao of Physics*

What is the purpose that has put the seeker on this road? To learn, certainly. To grow. To find an answer? To discover the truth about a rumored secret discipline which offers prowess, domination, invulnerability? To become one with the power and grace of the tiger, the speed and cleverness of the serpent, to soar with the eagle?

One can come here for many reasons. What will be found is a different matter. I'm going to describe one ultimate scenario. It is my own. It may not be entirely yours.

Looking to act out the character of the quintessential martial artist, I strive to become that person in reality. This is what I find.

The titles of these following passages are intended only as punctuation, devices put here as a way to divide the material into easy to find, readable chunks, not as headings or categories, not as a table of contents, or a description of the sections. These concepts are, as they were born to be, threaded together in a freely associative, mutually interacting progression. No one of these themes can be defined exclusively or separately. The ideas and the essays are inextricably woven together and feed each other.

*The sage takes
care of all men
And abandons
no one.
He takes care of
all things,
And abandons
nothing.
This is called
"following the
light."*
Lao tzu

CHIEN:
THE TEACHER

Reaching to Heaven. Creative, strong, the leader.

When the student ceases to be totally self-involved, interested in his own growth only, he will begin to turn to helping others. It is my opinion that at this point, regardless of prowess, the student becomes a true disciple. When this happens, a whole new vista of possibilities will appear.

Reaching out to help the poorer student, one will find answers to one's own weaknesses. Unfortunates living in an agony of unfulfillment respond dramatically to learning stimuli, and they are so grateful.

Sifu will immediately perceive this change and accelerate his teachings, beginning to reveal the mysteries; though, I must stress, there truly are no secrets. There are only inner techniques which seem simple and obvious once learned, and newer and deeper ways of seeing and feeling which clarify and enhance what we already know, propelling us to greater capacities.

This aspect of reaching out and helping those beneath us is a vital part of kung fu training. Without it, there is no way a new student can learn, and no way we can go on. The art would die and there would be no future.

Think of this: every student longs to be like the Master. What does the Master do? He teaches.

One can study and study for years, hours and hours every day, and one may still remain a student. To leap beyond the barrier one must break the chain. Stop practicing and start doing. Most will accomplish this by fighting, either informally or in competition. Not the best way—a great fighter will be an arrogant Master.

Some will progress through exhibition, that is, performing—presenting the styles as though they were dances, little ballets of combat. This makes for enormous grace and prettiness, but obsession with this path leads to something soft and almost effeminate, and without much depth or substance. On the other hand, everything furthers. A weak or misguided attempt is better than nothing. Failure is a lesson in itself.

The best way to break through is to teach. The most profound and substantial of the Masters are that way because they teach, because what they care about is not their own glory but the enlightenment of their fellow man.

To be complete, one must do everything: study, practice, fight, dance, meditate. But it all must come to teaching. The sage who keeps his council to himself is of no use to others. Whether he can see it or not, he is not that much use to himself either.

The lessons are not much good unless you can remember them. Teaching will build your ability to remember. I discovered that if I stepped away from the daily, or at least weekly, routine of practicing my forms, I would gradually forget. Time and again I would have to relearn things I had known perfectly some time before. Sifu told me then, "Take a pupil. Teach someone the moves, and you will never forget them again."

KUN:
THE HEALER

≡≡ ≡≡

The Earth power: devoted, receptive, soothing, selfless.

We have seen that the Master needs to reach out to others, to be helpful, and a force for good. This helpfulness can take many forms. With the power that comes with the teachings, great things can be accomplished. The knowledge and techniques that put the warrior in the center of the flow can be used to do the same thing for others. The heightened awareness and sense of rightness which the student has developed can be activated to diagnose and adjust the out-of-synch aspects of people, animals, things, and even events, conditions and situations.

Your chi can absolutely reach into and heal bodies and minds and spirits. There's no doubt about it. The same power that can defend and harm can soothe and rebuild. The *dim mak,* known as the "touch of death," wherein an apparently casual touch can prove fatal (one of the theories about the death of Bruce Lee), is actually a perversion of a technique which is intended to be used for healing. It is a measure of the misinformation surrounding the art that the technique is famous only for its killing power, while the healing aspect remains virtually unknown.

In traditional Japanese karate, I am told, the fifth degree *dan* is actually a medical degree. The same is true in the more loosely structured Way of kung fu. Before going further ahead in his studies, one must learn a healing art: acupuncture, acupressure, herb therapy and reflexology are popular choices. The idea is, in a nut shell, that if you are going to go around breaking people, you had better be able to put them back together.

Sifu Kam Yuen, at one point, closed the kwoon, gave up his businesses and enrolled in college for the study of chiropractics. He completed the course, served an internship and obtained his license. During this period, he studied pressure points and kinesiology as well, and augmented the knowledge of nutrition and vitamin and herb therapy which he had been developing for years. After completing his studies he opened a new school, complete with chiropractic clinic and vitamin and herb center, naming it "Shaolin West," which is associated with the Shaolin monastery in Northern China. Now you can take a class and get healed all in one visit. Sifu has taken to lining up the students after a class and giving to each one an individual adjustment and nutritional recommendation.

This doctoring which the Master takes up is bound to extend to healing of the mind and spirit.

Soothing, smoothing, uplifting, pushing and pulling the desperate, sad or confused disciple through the muck and mire towards tranquility and ease, not to mention enlightenment. It's all part of the job.

CHEN: THE WARRIOR

The arousing thunder. Always moving. Sudden and quick. Ambitious.

The true warrior is not merely a superb fighting machine. He needs to confront and overcome much more than mere opponents. He must triumph over adversities, philosophical stumbling blocks, spiritual trials, emotional crises, social and cosmic injustice, his own weakness, and possibly the devil himself. To accomplish all this our warrior would have to be a round person, highly evolved and armed with knowledge and insight.

The first goal, long before any kind of triumph, would be survival. The warrior must be correct. Always and absolutely. One mistake on the high wire could mean death. Precision then. Alertness. Realism. Illusion would be fatal. One would need perfect concentration and awareness of everything around at the same time.

Speed would be an essential. In movement and in thought.

Thought would have to extend into the future. Traps would be there which, walked into, allowed no escape. I've heard it said that in chess one must think at least three moves ahead. I think it's more like one must see the whole game, all its possible outcomes.

Moving deeper into the game, mere survival is, of course, not enough. No defensive posture, however effective, can succeed for long. Eventually it will be penetrated. It has been said the best defense is a good offense. True enough to some extent. It might not always work, though. That technique lacks caution. What if the other guy, or guys, are quick and tough, too. The way to go at it is to think: what is he doing? Why is he doing it? What can I do about it? And act. All of this applies not just to a physical confrontation, but to the whole range of life experiences you may have to deal with.

The warrior must know when to withdraw and when to attack. When to leave it alone and when to finish it.

Apply all this to a lawsuit, or a board meeting, a bicycle race or an argument with your wife. It's all just as relevant. The world is not ruled by muscles, it's ruled by brains.

The warrior must always do the unexpected. Heraclitus said that it is impossible to step in the same river twice because each time it is a different river. A later sage said you can't even step in the same river once, since it is changing as you step in it. A warrior must be like the river. He should never be found in the same place once.

Total commitment is required of the true warrior. He must be ready to be hurt, to lose, perhaps to die, willingly, even joyously. He's likely to be perfectly willing, with the same joyousness, to maim or kill.

A warrior's most valuable asset is his code. Whatever that may be, he must have it and be true to it. He who has no code is an animal. Every warrior has his code.

If a man tells you he has no code, that truly he is his own master, then his master is Satan and we know how to deal with *him*. Honor. Virtue. Even the devil has his code. Satan and his slaves cannot bear up in the face of virtue. Absolute honor destroys Satan's power absolutely.

In some old Norse paintings of Viking warriors, a strange character can be seen. Muscled like a champion body builder, he stands before the mast, with his arms folded, a sword in each hand, a round shield strapped to his back, little or no armor. Bare-chested

*The only
strategy which
an opponent
cannot predict is
a random
strategy.*
The Theory of
Games

*And your body
will flow
with the winds
of their hatred
And you will
take them
to the
destruction they
seek*
ninjitsu poem

and bare-armed and legged, wearing basically nothing but jewelry, and a huge grin on his face, at once innocent and fierce, he waits for the only moment he cares about in life: death in battle. This entity is known as "the berserker."

In Norse mythology, when a Viking dies in battle he goes straight to Valhalla, provided he has been in life kind to at least one woman, for it is she who must guide him there.

There is a story about one famous berserker. The Swedes were about to do battle, to prevent the taking of an important bridge by the advancing Danes. They were at dinner when the berserker came running in with news that the enemy was almost at the bridge. The Swedes liked their food and drink. They said, "All right. We'll be along as soon as we're finished."

The berserker said, "I'll go and hold them back until you get there, but don't be too long. I don't want to kill them all and leave nothing for you." He kissed the girls tenderly, then ran off and proceeded to hold the bridge, fighting off scores of soldiers.

When the Swedes had finished their coffee, they showed up. They found him standing on a pile of dead Danes, hacking away at the rest of them with great zeal.

When the berserker saw the Swedes, he shouted with glee, threw away his swords, tore off his shield and, arms wide open, leaped straight into the enemy host, deliberately impaling himself on their swords, and died joyously, having assured himself a hero's welcome in Valhalla.

Kung fu may not be the road for this berserker, or that ninja poet. Their attitudes are too specialized to make use of the wide knowledge contained in our teachings. Actually, the teachings might blunt the force of this simple-minded approach, weakening the Hell soldier to the point of ineffectiveness.

The exercise of extreme prejudice is not in keeping with the oneness with nature, spirituality, compassion and restraint that are a large part of the Shaolin mystique. The crusher doesn't need or can't use kung fu, and kung fu doesn't need the crusher. We demand something more from our warrior.

If this hasn't put you off, read on, tough guy.

KAN: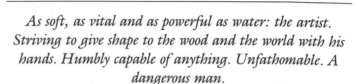
THE ARTISAN

As soft, as vital and as powerful as water: the artist. Striving to give shape to the wood and the world with his hands. Humbly capable of anything. Unfathomable. A dangerous man.

The true Master must be capable of taking hold of things. He needs to touch, to shape and to mold. Create, repair. It's not going to be enough to stand around kicking and dancing and then quietly vibing on the infinite. He has to *do* something. Not just his job, or an activity, something that brings him into visceral contact with how *it* works.

So, make a table, prune a tree, frame a picture. Paint a picture. Now we're talking.

The true Master is always proficient in the gentle arts as well as the fierce ones. This is a well-known fact. The neophyte looking for prowess in battle may think this is irrelevant elitist bull. Think again.

The great warriors were and are all poets, philosophers, musicians and artists. Alexander the Great, Richard the Lion-Hearted, William the Conqueror, Peter the Great, Charlemagne, Sun Gy and King Arthur, to name just a few, were all artists, musicians and mystics, as well as conquerors.

All the great samurai followed artistic pursuits, usually flower arranging or origami, the art of making flowers and birds out of folded paper. It may sound silly, but you'll have to at least give it a stab.

The principles of graphic arts: drawing, calligraphy, painting and sculpture, are real things. Structure, form and line are mathematical truths. Taste has little to do with it. Color is measured in wavelengths, and can be used to identify the atomic elements in distant stars. Study of these principles is absolutely required for a man of knowledge.

It is easy to begin a life of art. Start with appreciation. Go an art gallery or a bookstore. Find an artist you like and just look at his work. Read about his life. The rest will follow naturally. Sculpture is particularly interesting to any athlete because of its tactile portrayal of the human body in motion.

Take a pen or pencil, or a piece of chalk or crayon, and begin. Just daub a color on the paper or canvas. Do it strictly for yourself, not to impress anyone else. Work as large as you can so it won't get fussy. The easiest things to draw and paint are flowers, and the softness and delicacy of them helps to create a good balance for the martial artist.

Sculpture begins with a piece of clay. Push and scrape and twist the clay into something you like. Stay away from tools at first; your hands are always your best tools. Use subjects that interest you to increase your enthusiasm. Art is joy.

I have known a warrior who, with no previous experience, made a house with his own mind and hands. It is perhaps the most beautiful house I have ever seen. Courageous, strong, inspiring. He began it with a pile of sticks and a barrel of nails.

KEN: THE SAGE

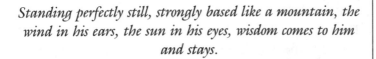

Standing perfectly still, strongly based like a mountain, the wind in his ears, the sun in his eyes, wisdom comes to him and stays.

The Master is possessed of wisdom. Flowing with events, unperturbed by adversity, one with nature, divested of most human problems. This state is more a question of attitude than of knowledge. Knowing without knowing, with the gaps filled in by information, if one needs to stoop so low.

Going with the flow is a more dynamic commitment than it sounds. The position of the leaf that drifts effortlessly through the rapids is precisely correct at all times.

By opening the temple within you to the will of the One Thing, you are putting yourself right in the center of the Flow. The entire sweep of the past, present and future, and all the separate realities and alternate universes are arrayed around you like constellations which, as one with them, you control. You don't flow through it any more than it flows through you. This is a big part of the meaning of the designation "Master."

Deliberately striving to become a sage probably won't work. Remember that this path may only be found by one who knows without knowledge, and has not come seeking the One Thing he seeks.

In Taoist terms, the One Thing refers to the central power of the universe, the will of the cosmos, the one force which governs, predicts and impels the Ten Thousand Things, which is to say: the whole of creation, the events, places, tenants and paraphernalia, the whole range of experience, consciousness and personality, the whole thing, the universe; the Ten Thousand Things, which are the reflection of the One Thing, and which form it, in the same act.

In Taoist thinking, as in quantum mechanics, actions cannot be perceived, only participated in. The eye that is observing is part of the design.

When the *I Ching* is consulted, the book falls open and reveals what it cannot help but reveal, because it is One with the One Thing. This same stance is the one thing that the warrior must achieve to become the sage.

You're looking for a miracle, to break down the wall, perceive the cosmos outside, to be part of a unifying and expanding, gathering force that will take us away to a truly creative existence, unfettered by matter, error, mortality. The whole of society is set up to prevent this. We are asked to adjust, to conform, to settle, when wide open cosmic awareness is what we seek.

Focus on the here and now. Watch. Listen. Be good, however it is you define good. Try to understand. Rise above desire and need. Don't look for personal gain. You might just find yourself there. You'll know when it happens.

A sojourn on a mountain top is a tried and true approach. So is a season in Hell.

SUN:
THE MUSICIAN

Gentle, penetrating, the entire sweet and terrible story of Creation can be heard whispering and roaring in the wind, rustling in the leaves. All held in place and bursting forth from his fingers on the lute.

Power to soothe the savage beast. Music is not just one of life's pleasantries—the laws of harmonics are some of the most basic in our universe. Many people think music is an art form created by Man. This is not exactly true. The notes of our scales are based on the actual resonances of the cosmos. This can be scientifically demonstrated.

The elements, the planets and the stars vibrate at specific frequencies. These resonances are what define the differences and similarities in all things, animate and inanimate.

The Hopi, Zuni and Navajo use music and dancing in their rituals as a way for healing and to improve conditions and generally put things right. These rituals are called "sings," and usually take several days to perform. They are guarded against casual use, which is considered sacreligious, being revealed only at times of need—with names like "The Blessing Way" and "Dance of She Woman Forever Not Change." Only four times has this Hopi dance ever been necessary. Four times when the Many Worlds were all in danger.

The eight houses and the sixty-four hexagrams of the *I Ching,* and the traditional sixty-four positions of kung fu are mirrored in the eight notes of the octave. The rotation of the planets can be heard in the twelve-tone scale.

Music is structure. Giving form and substance to the naked air. Held together with harmony and released by melody, it reaches everywhere.

Playing an instrument is a way of examining the fabric of the universe with your own fingers, and coming to understand some of its basic structure; a way in which these realities can be experienced directly. This is a much more profound approach to assimilating kung fu principles than trying to outguess an opponent, and will help one to do that as well.

Learning to tune your instrument teaches even more; and building an instrument yourself will bring the lesson all the way home.

The guitar is the easiest instrument to play and the hardest to learn. Its positions and combinations give themselves easily to storytelling. The piano keyboard contains an entire orchestra all arranged in a neat line. Simple and tremendous. These two instruments stand alone. The wind instruments, flutes, saxophones, trumpets, can only play the melody. They need to get together to play the big stuff, but they can soar and scream. Strings such as the violin or cello are hellishly difficult from the beginning to the end— some people like a challenge. Drums are sheer power, measured and wild, tigers on a leash. You need a bass on the bottom. Can't build far without a foundation.

All the instruments evolve from five primitive ideas. Blasting air into the horn of an animal: "toot." Blowing into a hollow reed with holes in it for the fingers: "whistle." Twanging on a taut bow-string:

"plunk." And beating on something with hands or sticks: "boom." All of the raw materials for these instruments are to be found beside the road, or in the shoulder bag of the hunter-warrior.

The fifth instrument is the human voice, which is capable of imitating all the others. Crying out loud, yelling, crooning, growling. The singer. Nothing cheers one up so much as singing out loud. Do it in the shower, of course, but how about while driving your car, climbing stairs, making breakfast, sweeping the courtyard of the temple? Many of the monks are known to hum along as an accompaniment to the workout.

Not knowing music is like not knowing how to swim. There's no reason for it except neglect, best corrected. Some people will say they have no ear for music. Take heart, the aptitude can be developed. Believe me, there is really no such thing as tone-deafness. If one can hear, one can learn to differentiate notes. Like anything else, it's just a question of learning how. And, anyway, the music doesn't have to be "in tune." We're after cosmic awareness, not a career in rock'n roll.

Music is God talking. Listen to the wind. You will hear the song of the elements, the planets, the stars and of your own heart.

LI:
THE POET

Clinging to thoughts and words, giving light to the darkness, shining like the sun, crackling with fire. The poet. The bard.

To maximize the benefits of kung fu study, you have to reach for the stars. Only a poet can do that.

To be a poet doesn't mean just to write poems. It's much grander than that. Seeing and appreciating the beauty and grace in things—as well as the horror, the sadness. Putting it all together in a meaningful way. Truth through feeling. Metaphors, parables. Making difficult ideas easier to understand. A hawk plunging down the sky to take his prey, a deer stepping timidly into a meadow, a horse rearing, an old grandfather fishing on a bank with his grandson, the bloody death of a bullfighter, the song of a bird; it's all poetry. The man, who is alert to it all, and knows it, is a poet.

With the poet comes the muse.

The man of action contemplates the muse, and discovers the poetry in his soul. This can take many forms. For some the muse is a real live person, for others a force of spirit, the Moon, a gold medallion, the Holy Mother Mary, a mirror. Everybody's different. I personally prefer a live, warm, vibrating and supportive woman with the face of an angel and a body made for loving, who whispers her inspiration in my ear along with the sweet nothings and lusty suggestions, but sometimes I'm inspired by something less easy to grab.

I once knew a mad philosopher whose muse seemed to be a wooden Indian. One day his brother got mad at him and burned it up. He dried up and couldn't write. It takes all kinds.

The muse can be difficult at times: demanding, unresponsive, selfish, jealous, bitchy. Sometimes it requires coaxing to convince the muse to bring out in us the poetry that is in the air.

There's poetry everywhere. You simply have to look or listen to find it. The dances of kung fu are full of poetry in motion. It's not enough to be fast, accurate, forceful. You have to be graceful, supple, complex, subtle and profound as well. The flowing moves, the rhythms, the dazzling reverses that make kung fu effective and therapeutic are poetic as all hell.

This rhythm, power and grace can and will extend itself into the rest of the warrior's life without any special effort or intention. The mind and the muscles, once awakened, will not shut down when you leave the gym floor. You'll see it in your golf or tennis game, on the ski slope, sailing your boat or flying your plane.

Every step you take will have in it the essence of your new knowledge. Reaching for the salt, running for the bus, driving your car, painting your fence, writing a letter or brushing your hair, the poetry will be there. You'll walk like a tiger, float like a dragon, strike with the speed and accuracy of the snake, stand like a tall tree, sleep and dream with the visions of a nine-year-old boy or a six-year-old girl.

If you want to turn this sense of poetry to specific use, it won't be hard to learn to appreciate or create little bits of it in your daydreams or activities. This is bound to enhance and add spice to your social and business relations, your work and play, and put a spark into your confrontations and adventures.

Most or all of the great philosophy is written down as some form of poetry. You might try it yourself. It isn't difficult. Anyone can write—making things up or just putting down events or feelings. Dreamy school children do it without any effort at all. You take an empty page and put something on it. Don't be shy. It doesn't have to be any good. Once it's down in black and white, you can change it, refine, edit; but you have to start with something. It doesn't take genius, just focus. Ideas will come to you out of nowhere. Words will flow easily.

If you can't see your way clear to doing all this, you needn't. Poetry is in the heart and in the air, not on a piece of paper. Practice your exercises, sharpen your senses, move with grace and power. If you are not the poet, you'll be the poem.

*What did the
Buddhist say to
the hot dog
vendor? Make
me One with
Everything,
please.*

*It's just a great
big cosmic joke.*
The Sage

TUI:
THE FOOL

*Filled with the joy of life, pure pleasure, spreading himself
across pain and sorrow like a lake of gladness, the clown
reigns supreme.*

No being or system is complete without a strong sense
of the humor of it all. No social unit can endure without its clown. No intelligent organism can abide a life
of utter seriousness. Laughter can cure many things:
arrogance, pain, fear, depression, anger, confusion,
perhaps even a broken heart. It is impossible to get a
complete picture of anything without the knowledge
that behind the most serious truths, the darkest misery, is a great big cosmic joke.

Maybe you don't get the point yet. Trust me, it's
there. Laugh anyway! Get in the habit, even if you
don't mean it. Sooner or later, the humor of it is
bound to come to you, and the laughter will become
real.

When it does, sorrow and trouble will fall away.
When the vultures start circling, the thought of how
silly they look will put things in a truer perspective. At
your worst moments you will find a spring in your
step and a song in your heart.

Laughter is caused by information going into the
"yes" and the "no" channels of the brain at the same
time. They meet in the middle and cause a short cir-
cuit; laughter releases the overload. At least that's my
theory. It feels better than sneezing and, like sneezing,
it clears the system.

The sage must comprehend, or at least acknowl-
edge, the paradox of life on Earth, apprehending and
savoring the ridiculousness of any situation. He will
be especially liberal in heaping laughter on himself.
Guaranteed to clear the air. Try it. The wonderful
relief it gives to those around you is, in itself, worth
the whole exercise.

Remember that part of the sage's bag of tricks is the paradox factor. When he's given everything to learn the true meaning, he finds out the opposite is true as well. If that isn't funny, I don't know what is.

One reason why the writings of the great mystics are full of paradox and trick answers is the joke factor. Observation of the true nature of things always results in laughter. Understanding the cosmos has a lot of humor connected with it. Once you get the great big cosmic joke it's hard to stop laughing—everything that goes on on this planet seems really funny.

It's not enough to just laugh. You have to *be* the fool. Gazing at the sky, ready to step off a cliff, without knowing it. It's part of letting yourself go. The cosmos cannot intervene in your case unless you surrender your senses. The original meaning of the word "silly" was "holy" based on the idea that an idiot has a direct experience of God.

Step away from the normal and mundane and embrace the bizarre. If you don't see things differently, chances are you don't see things as they are.

So, amidst the wisdom, the beauty, the power and the fire, mix in a big dose of slapstick. Make faces, walk funny, roll your eyes. Dance, cavort, do magic tricks, talk nonsense. Be a clown!

MASTERY

The true study of any philosophy is to overcome ignorance and prejudice on the road to discovering the true purpose of mankind in relation to the real world and the design of the Maker—leading to effectiveness, tranquility, enlightenment and transcendence.

Taoist philosophy is based on the concept of oneness with nature, reverence for all things great and small, harmony and understanding.

Buddhist doctrine underlines progress through suffering ("The world is a house which is burning down"), through application and obedience, toward a goal of usefulness.

These, along with the old Hindu forms and metaphors and the rigors, theories and practices of martial combat, combine and explode into a dynamic, expanded, tempered and wild new Way: a Way of the hard and the soft, the spontaneous and the choreographed, the Fist and the Book. At one with the One Thing.

In the quest to know one's true measure, it is necessary to test oneself against adversarial forces and situations. Opponents must be confronted, I suppose, or it is all only a dance. However, once this path has been covered, further obsession with fighting becomes mere aggression, unbecoming to the true seeker.

The theater of martial arts is the magic lantern show: tournaments, exhibitions, demonstrations, dances. All are an entertaining way to continue the process of discovery. It doesn't matter how little these games have to do with actual combat or how irrelevant they seem to real situations; they still profit you. The gains in courage, confidence, grace and power are considerable, and the sweat is honest. They, in their way, foster the growth of an effective life system and lead to a path to the Way.

As the *I Ching* oracle tells it, "Everything furthers." The more elements you assimilate, the more effective the system, the more complete the picture.

Of course, if you are one of the chosen few who perceive the clear white light in the beginning and accept it, there is no need for these pursuits, though you might play with them just for the fun of it. For the rest of us, we need all the help we can get.

The knowledge, the skills and the strengths which a master has achieved must be used to turn aside wrath, promote tolerance, understanding, harmony and peace. This influence is the most valuable contribution a martial artist can make to the world. Its effect will spread out about him like the ever widening ripples in a pool, caused by the dropping of a pebble.

The image of a powerful man who uses his strength to nurture, teach and heal is irresistible.

To achieve this tranquil stance, a martial artist must sweep away anger, envy and vanity. The alternative leads to arrogance, oppression and domination. Tranquility is a candle in the wind. The slightest breath of violence or aggression can extinguish it.

Ultimately, the superior man will come to know that it is sometimes better to touch filth than to be filth. Unless this lesson is learned, progress will be limited. Stagnation, or something worse, will be the probable result.

Above all, the thing the Master must learn to master is himself.

In the end, there is nothing I can tell you which will lead you to the goal you seek. All these words are only the echoes of my own failure. If I could find my own Way, I would not be here to write this book for you.

Surpass me. Go on by yourself. Leave me. It is the only course. After all, I know nothing.

My usefulness is ended. You are the teacher now.

11

A WORD OF CAUTION

Supreme illumination is an arrow straight to hell.
Zen Roshi doctrine

Nothing is true. Everything is permitted.
Hashishan

 For most students initiation into the mysteries is not an entirely likable experience. True enlightenment is a radical goal, requiring great sacrifice and fearless abandon in its pursuit.

Realization of the goal can be devastating. You will discover knowledge which will change you forever. You may forsake your old ways and beliefs, turn your back on your old ambitions and goals, and lose the loves of your life.

Things which are tied down securely and ideas which hold water will survive, but impractical or useless artifacts, false or muddy concepts, questionable practices and sentimental attachments will be swept away or left behind. Expect the quest to break your heart at least once.

Be careful. You probably have no conception of what you are getting into. However, if you insist, in spite of this warning, in going on with your search, there are many compensations. Remember that what you choose is what you get. The future you will discover is the one you have sought in your quest, whether you know it or not.

You are both the sculptor and the clay. Seek danger and you will find it. Seek love, fulfillment, knowledge—whatever you most long for—the cost may be great, but you will find it all.

The quest for enlightenment is dangerous to the caterpillar, but essential to the butterfly.

12

GATHERING
THE POWER

*Something goes
wrong
every minute.
What you do is
fix it.*
Lt. Gen. Gus
Pagonis

*Shoes are the
hats of the feet;
and it is
difficult
to pray while
wearing a hat.*
Old Chinese
Proverb

Take all the elements we have described, and put them to use within yourself; you, the Seeker. Keep it simple. Stand humbly and proudly. Accept everything for what it is. Throw off the chains of your fears and limitations. Avoid prejudice and judgement. Strive. Persevere. Be creative, arousing, unfathomable, still; unmoving and moving, receptive, gentle and penetrating; cling to the light. Shine with the sun; be Joyous, giving and taking pleasure. Enjoy peace, tranquility. Smile through the tears. Fall down and get up again. Be gentle with yourself, while demanding the most from your body, your mind, your spirit and your soul. Accept no excuses. Search until you find. Welcome hardship. Do not avoid pain or difficulty, sorrow or heartbreak. Seek these things out if you dare. Teach yourself everything there is to know. Teach others everything you have learned. Be truthful, kind, helpful, giving, loving, faithful. Hold fast to your code, your ideals and your reputation. Hold to them unwaveringly. Avoid the evil, poisonous serpents of wrong-doing and dissipation, desire, obsession, excess and Destruction. Overcome sloth, vanity, envy, hatred, anger, gluttony, lust, jealousy, pettiness, greed, selfishness. Give up meanness; no bully can attain mastery. Revile the beast. Don't complain. The troubles you may have are merely mechanical; small and insignificant. They will pass. Be alone but never lonely. You are all things when you stand alone. Ask for nothing. Wait. The One Thing will provide. Don't be led astray. Be cautious and suspicious in your dealings; for there is much evil in the world. No one is safe from it. Beware of false friends, criminals, liars and cheats. Be trusting. Find the goodness in all things. Forgive the most terrible wrongs, but never forget. Turn your cheek again and again. Strike when it is called for. Strike quickly and with meaning. Don't be cruel. When you find true fellowship, welcome it and keep it sacred. Nothing is more real than lasting friendship. The cosmos revolves peacefully around the union that is true. We need each other. Watch carefully. Keep your ears open. Stay awake. Stop dreaming. Face reality; yet, indulge yourself in fantasy and fairy tales. Have and keep hope, faith, charity. Believe in your luck. Take chances. Realize your dreams. Seek enlightenment and give it. Help things to grow, within yourself and in the Ten Thousand Things. Walk softly, lightly. Try not to leave your mark on the land. Replace your divots. Move quietly, without racket, but let the world know you are passing through. Welcome strangers, assist travelers. Feed the hungry, and the homeless. Turn away the beggars. Be strong and stable; graceful and swift. Feel the power. Be cheerful and steady. Follow your heart. Smile, laugh. Sing freely, dance wildly; sit perfectly still and listen. The supreme power will speak. Do not doubt it. Find the center. Flow. Remember you can do nothing wrong. Ask every question. Question every answer. Answer every question and every answer with a question. Be One with the One Thing. No matter what may come, don't give up.

Go on, unflinchingly, with your QUEST.

Stone tablet of Ode to Bodhidharma, written by
Huang Tingjian.
From Shaolin Kung Fu *by Ying Zi and Weng Yi.*

APPENDIXES

MARTIAL ARTS
AROUND THE WORLD

Following are thumbnail sketches concerning the other martial arts systems (besides Northern Shaolin style kung fu) with which I am familiar. In no way should these observations be regarded as definitive. The knowledgeable will find inaccuracies. I am not an encyclopedia. Most of my information comes from casual conversations I have had with individual martial artists. Some of it has got to be pure rumor. Take it for what it is.

The Southern kung fu styles:
I have studied Hungar, Black Tiger, Tiger Crane, and certain protective, strengthening, expanding, curative and regenerative stances, moves and combinations related to the Southern styles. All this Southern training was liberally steeped in inner chi, expressed with great force, together with powerful external muscular strength, co-existing side by side with the chi.

My mentor in these styles was Silver Gordon. Silver is African-American, Native American and Chinese—and that's the way he fights, teaches and prescribes. He is about 6′5″ tall, lean and hard, and has very long arms and legs, and huge hands. He works fast and hard, with his three heritages very apparent in his method and style.

Along with the training went a constant rap about the training, about herbal cures; war stories concerning the life and times of a warrior teacher, at work and play, in the ghetto and on the street, as enforcer, bodyguard, lone wolf, security cop. Silver's information is very much outside the common pale. There is really no society where his ethnic make-up is to any extent welcomed.

I met Silver through a trumpet player—Kevin Peachey, a fine musician, who had been extremely proficient at tai kwondo until he embraced kung fu, largely as a result of his contact with me. Silver managed to completely convert him. Peach now teaches kung fu when he's not touring with his band.

Silver introduced me to a number of herbs and herbal combinations I had never heard of, and added to the knowledge that I already had about others. Some of these formulas Silver revealed, and some he only administered. Sometimes he would prescribe something and I would learn by the label he fastened to the bag or jar.

Jui Jitsu:

Jui jitsu means "grabbing." The fame of jui jitsu in the Western world dates back to its use by American commandos during the Second World War. It is a Japanese style derived from Chinese chen na, or "grabbing techniques." Every kung fu system has these chen na techniques. Jui jitsu simply concentrates on them more exclusively. As this style evolved it became characterized by a certain brutality. One doesn't simply grab—one grabs, throws and twists, wrenches. Jui jitsu tournaments have become rare because of their reputation for commonly ending with broken or shattered arms and legs. Today it is taught more as a defense against rapists and muggers than anything else.

Judo:

A derivation of jui jitsu which confines itself to basically one technique—that of using the opponent's force to his disadvantage. Primarily, it consists of re-directing the aggressive energy of an assailant into a fall or immobility. Judo was the first martial art to be taught in colleges in the United States.

Karate:

A Japanese system derived, of course, from kung fu; adapted to fit the peculiarities of Japanese culture, custom and ideology—most of which were also evolved from Chinese models. The differences are predictable: flashy, monolinear, specifically limited to no-nonsense techniques yielding immediate results. Training is highly structured, ritualistic and rigorous to the point of ordeal, and extremely competitive.

Tai kwondo:

Defined as Korean karate. The development of systems on the mainland of Asia, however, generally predate the development on the islands.

Aikido:

A form of tai kwondo in which, it is said, one avoids humiliating or humbling the opponent, or otherwise causing him to "lose face"—while at the same time more or less destroying him. Violent action with honorific ritual attached.

Hapkido:

A system which seems to concentrate on doing the greatest amount of damage in the shortest amount of time, bringing the fight to a brutal end as quickly as possible. Typically, when a hapkido practitioner strikes a blow, he continues striking until the opponent is prostrate, broken and unconscious, perhaps dead. Its most characteristic aspect is the insistent intrusion on the opponent's space—a technique ideally suited for a Northern Shaolin or, to a certain extent, a judo defense; both of which stress the invitation of intrusive aggression, the energy of which is then turned against the opponent.

Tang soo do:

A regional variation of tai kwondo, made famous as the style of Chuck Norris.

Kempo:

Karate variation known to America as an importation from Hawaii. Brought here and promoted here by Ed Parker, its popularity largely resulting from Elvis Presley's involvement with Parker.

Shotokai:

Karate variation created in Tokyo around 1926. It tries to elevate karate from a sport into an art of living.

Sumo:

Tournament style wherein two enormously large combatants strive by grappling to throw down each other, or cause the other to step out of the arena, pretty much through sheer force of mass. Essentially a game of "King of the Mountain." It is said that in the ancient (presently banned) imperial tournaments, the winner would present the loser's heart or, at the very least, two or three ribs to the emperor.

Ninjitsu:

The art of the assassin; an esoteric discipline, shrouded in secrecy; employing special tools, tricks, drugs and poisons; techniques of invisibility and subterfuge; hypnotism and torture. A good deal of occult and paranormal aspects are associated with this mysterious cult. The system makes use of bits and pieces from all sorts of other disciplines, such as wall climbing with equipment and chemistry and acrobatics. Divided into two main schools—the Red and the Black—whose differences are largely a matter of ideology.

Savatte:

Essentially French kick boxing, not, however, derived from Asian beginnings—a coincidental similarity to them consisting only in the use of the feet.

Bojitsu:

Staff or wand. Similar to quarter staff. Common to all systems.

Philippine stick fighting:

A very effective technique within the Philippine system using two wooden sticks about twenty-two inches long. The islanders were able to defeat the superiorly armed Spanish for one hundred years with these sticks. One of their favorite tricks was to break the wrist of a swordsman, rendering him helpless. Philippine stick fighting is now included in many of the martial arts programs. All of the systems are taught with stick fighting as one of the techniques, in at least some of the schools. In others, though the technique is not taught in the classes, it is practiced; passed around by the students to themselves; just as, although no purist kung fu Master is likely to teach *num chucks* in his kwoon, they'll be around.

Conversely, you will now find Philippine fighters who are versed in several of the arts.

Another weapon of the Philippines which has become quite widespread is the butterfly knife, which is toyed with by martial artists and street punks everywhere. The bolo, roughly equivalent to the machete, is the work knife of the coconut forests; coming in many sizes and styles, the bolo can be found at the waist of most rural islanders. The steel used in these blades is mostly cut from engine blocks and axle shafts. The bolo can be wielded as an axe, club, sword, razor, screwdriver, scalpel, hammer or crowbar; instantly convertible from tool to weapon.

Samurai:

An ancient Japanese sword-fighting discipline. Soldiers, outlaws, warlords, politicians, teachers, saviors, doctors, priests and saints—the samurai were a whole stratum of society, a cult, a class, a political power; a force for good or evil, the established order and the outcasts.

The two swords and the dagger are as basic to Japanese custom and tradition as the hunting rifle and buck knife are to ours. The short sword is the one used for *hara-kiri,* the ritual suicide. The incision is made with the point; a fairly strong push to penetrate the muscle sheath, and then a slow entry, followed by a cut to the side, and a long cut up. The longer the process can be stretched out, the greater the honor.

A friend or comrade in arms acts as a second; standing ready to cut off the head with the long sword, should there be any sign of dishonorable faltering. If the ritual is completed successfully, with the sword replaced on its stand, the head lowered, exposing the neck, the second then cuts the head off anyway; hopefully with one blow, though sometimes it is known to take two or three.

Shogun:

Medieval Japanese system predating and in virtually all ways similar to samurai.

Wu shu:

At the start of the Cultural Revolution, kung fu, being a religious discipline, a revolutionary force and an imperial relic, was outlawed. In order to fill the gap, a non-secular form of dancing was created. Using modern clothes and shoes, played out as a dance, the moves are acrobatic and graceful, having not necessarily any relevance to fighting techniques.

The wu shu dances are also presented as a game; with interlocking forms which, when performed simultaneously by two or more subjects, become interactive, choreographed combat pieces. All the weapons are included. There is supposedly no sanctioned sparring or actual fighting. Wu shu is mainly for show, and a show it is. Soaring, leaping, sliding, twirling, with great flexibility, power, agility, height and distance, and a certain amount of dramatic emotional content. Colorful and broad. Usually done to music.

Practiced daily in public squares throughout China by people of all walks of life and all ages, in massed groups of tens of thousands.

The drunken technique:

Common to many systems, this style makes use of the loose, spontaneous, lucky, sloppy moves of a drunk to achieve unexpected rhythm and flow in a fight; sometimes as a subterfuge, as in a surprise attack; and sometimes as a straight technique, or out of arrogance or as a joke. Many teachers and practitioners scoff at this style as corny and undignified. It is a good defense against street gangs; it's possible to maim or at least temporarily immobilize several assailants before the aggressors realize you're not just accidentally bumping into people and backhanding others out of sheer awkwardness. When they catch on, you can "wake up" and take care of their depleted ranks with all your faculties revealed and in use.

Old man techniques:

As the body grows old, certain changes occur. Strengths of a certain kind increase or appear, while others fade and vanish. Speed lessens in some ways, while in others time seems to stretch, allowing a casual easy rhythm. Certain kinds of movement become difficult. New techniques are introduced to compensate for and capitalize on these changes. An old man's kick does not stress the ligaments, but still can smash doors and knock out walls. With the special ability to stretch time that the old kung fu man has within any given moment, he has the leisure to set in place subtle techniques: grabbing and pulling, focusing, inserting, turning, touching; compelling the outcome with his considerable chi power.

Wrestling, kick boxing, competition karate, prize fighting:

These are all techniques which require a set of rules that limit the techniques which are allowed. They are all restricted to victory within certain bounds. They have their place, and are legitimate tests, but are not, nor do they pretend to be truly ultimate fighting styles: nor do they bother with the larger questions of philosophy, religion and art that the true martial arts stress as part of their litany.

Muhammud Ali, at his prime, once said that in a real street fight he would be in a lot of trouble.

True kung fu fighting is pure street fighting. Get the job done in the most direct possible way. Still, the student who stresses this aspect and ignores the philosophy and all the rest will never achieve prowess, and will miss his heart's desire, never achieving enlightenment. Note the fact that practitioners of all forms of fighting, who have won titles, and beaten everyone around, find themselves worn and broken has-beens at the end.

A philosopher, on the other hand, becomes a teacher and a leader, and continues to work effectively until he dies.

Tai chi chuan, pa kua, and hsing:

These are the three main Soft or Internal Systems, based on chi; of which tai chi, or tai chi chuan, is the most well known. These systems are a triumph of the techniques of softness, flowing with the stream, calm assurance and chi power. They are practiced mainly by old people and women; however, they are as effective as any hard technique, and considerably less destructive.

The movements of pa kua are founded directly on the principles of the eight trigrams and the sixty-four hexagrams of the *I Ching*.

A tai chi, pa kua or hsing fighter (if you can even use that word to describe these holy sages) is pretty much unbeatable, though this may never become a proven fact through domination. A Master will simply never be in trouble, never be hurt.

Opponents are likely to stumble away in confusion, uncertain of their feelings, and unaware that any contest took place. Most hsing or pa kua victories occur before the fight begins. Tai chi disciples prefer to spend their time breathing deeply and watching the sun rise.

The slow movements of these internal systems are boring to most young martial arts students, which is their loss. "Typical of the impatience of youth, and of the modern world in general!" the old tai chi Master might say.

No problem. The youngster will grow into it somewhere along the way, if he lasts that long. Someone once said that the tragedy of youth is that it is wasted on the young. The tragedy of tai chi chuan, hsing and pa kua is that they are wasted on the old. We could all profit greatly from the intense concentration of chi alone. The young and quick always think they know better.

Time wasted is time lost. Lost time cannot really be made up for. Still, no blame. *Now* is all the time there really is. It's all happening at once. Everything furthers.

FILMOGRAPHY

Films by David Carradine which contain or are concerned with the martial arts. Most of these are available on video.

Kung Fu, 1971–75
Death Race 2000, 1975
Thunder and Lightning, 1976
Cannonball, 1976
Deathsport, 1978
Circle of Iron, 1979
Lone Wolf McQuade, 1983
The Warrior and the Sorceress, 1984
P.O.W. the Escape, 1986
Kung Fu, the Movie (TV), 1986
Armed Response, 1986
Open Fire, 1987
Animal Protectors, 1988
Warlords, 1988
Wizards of the Lost Kingdom II, 1989
Future Force, 1989
Try This One for Size, 1989
Future Zone, 1990
Gambit, 1990
Martial Law, 1990
Dune Warrior, 1991
Kung Fu, The Legend Continues, 1993

. . . so far.

BIBLIOGRAPHY

The smallest sampling of related reading and viewing material.

Capra, Fritjof. *The Tao of Physics*. Boston: Shambhala, 1983.

Carradine, David. *Kung Fu Workout* (video). Time Life Videos.

———. *Tai Chi Workout* (video). Tai Mantis Productions.

Castaneda, Carlos. *The Teachings of Don Juan*. Berkeley: University of California Press, 1968.

Confucius. *The Great Digest, The Unwobbling Pivot, The Analects*. Translated by Ezra Pound. New York: New Directions, 1969.

Gibran, Kahlil. *The Prophet*. New York: A.A. Knopf, 1978.

Gurdjieff, George Ivanovitch. *View From the Real World*. New York: E.P. Dutton & Co., Inc., 1973.

Hesse, Hermann. *Siddhartha*. Translated by Hilda Rosner. New York: New Directions, 1951.

Hua, Ellen Kei, ed. *Kung Fu Meditations*. Ventura: Thor Publishing Company, 1974.

Lee, Bruce. *The Tao of Jeet Kune Do*. Burbank: O'Hara, 1975.

Neihardt, John G. *Black Elk Speaks*. University of Nebraska Press, 1988.

Ouspensky, P.D. *The Fourth Way*. New York: Random House, 1971.

———. *In Search of the Miraculous*. San Diego: Harcourt Brace Jovanovich Inc., 1965.

Rampa, T. Lobsang. *The Third Eye*. New York: Ballantine Books, Inc., 1986.

Shea, Robert and Wilson, Robert Anton. *Illuminatus! Trilogy: The Eye in the Pyramid, The Golden Apple & Leviathan*. New York: Dell Publishing Co., Inc., 1984.

Szekely, Edmund. *Essene Gospel of Peace*. San Diego: IBS
    International, 1981.
Tolkien, J.R.R. *Lord of the Rings*. Boston: Houghton Mif-
    flin Co., 1986.
Tsu, Lao. *Tao Te Ching*. Translated by Gia-fu Feng and Jane
    English. New York: Vintage Books, 1972.
Tzu, Chuang. *Inner Chapters*. Edited by Gia-fu Feng. Trans-
    lated by Jane English. New York: Vintage Books,
    1974.
Wei Wu Wei. *All Else Is Bondage*.
Yi, Weng and Zi, Ying. *Shaolin Kung Fu*. Hong Kong:
    Kingsway International Publications, 1981.
Yuen, Kam. *Beginning Kung Fu*. Burbank: O'Hara.
———. *Three Sectional Staff*. Burbank: O'Hara.